W9-AQG-193

The
Mezzaluna
Cookbook

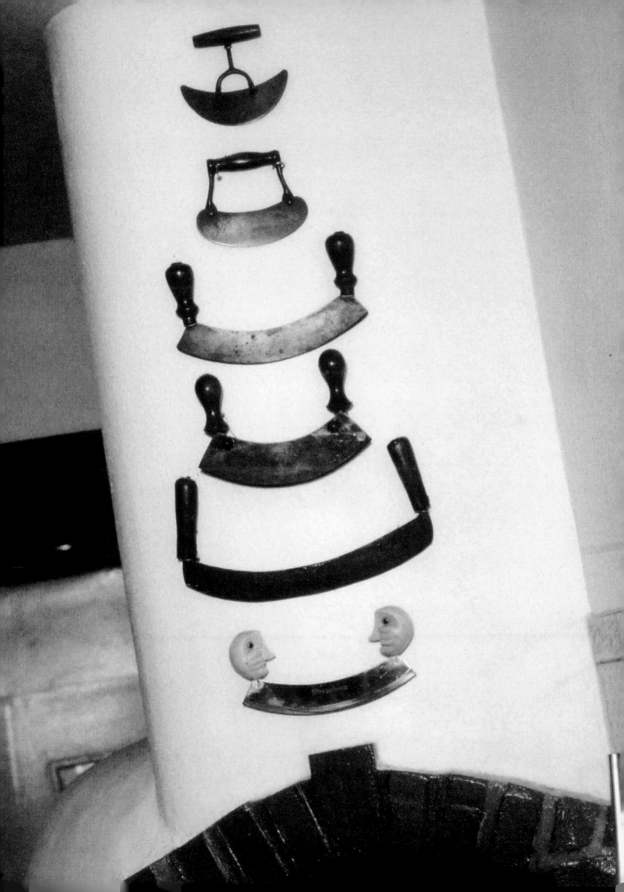

The Mezzaluna
Cookbook

Over 100 Recipes for Seasonal Pastas,

Pizzas, Carpaccios, and More

ALDO BOZZI AND ISABEL BAU MADDEN

Photographs by Vladimir A. Lennox

Clarkson Potter/Publishers

New York

To the memory of my father, Enrico, who always
believed in my food projects —A.B.

Copyright © 1995 by Aldo Bozzi and Isabel Bau Madden
Photographs copyright © 1995 by Vladimir A. Lennox
Artwork by Lorenzo Pezzatini (page 7), Mario Lo Vergine (page 36),
Angelo Formichella (page 51), and Silvia Marilli (page 99)
copyright © 1984 Mezzaluna. Used by permission.

All rights reserved. No part of this book may be reproduced or transmitted in any form or by any
means, electronic or mechanical, including photocopying, recording, or by any information storage
and retrieval system, without permission in writing from the publisher.

Published by Clarkson N. Potter, Inc., 201 East 50th Street, New York, New York 10022. Member of
the Crown Publishing Group.

Random House, Inc. New York, Toronto, London, Sydney, Auckland

CLARKSON N. POTTER, POTTER, and colophon are trademarks of Clarkson N. Potter, Inc.

Manufactured in the United States of America

Design by Louise Fili

Library of Congress Cataloging-in-Publication Data
Bozzi, Aldo.
The Mezzaluna cookbook/Aldo Bozzi and Isabel Bau Madden.
Includes index.
1. Cookery (Pasta) 2. Cookery, Italian. I. Madden, Isabel Bau. II. Title.
TX809.M17B69   1995
641.8'22—dc20   95-30338

ISBN 0-517-70181-2

10   9   8   7   6   5   4   3   2   1

First Edition

Acknowledgments

THANK YOU TO: Chiara, for all her patience and help; my great chef, Paolo Casagranda, for his assistance and precious suggestions throughout the entire project; my skillful "pizzaiolo" Francesco Vitale; Peter Vega and the entire team at Mezzaluna in New York; my chefs Ugo Alesina at Mezzaluna in Corona del Mar and Stefano Bosetti at Mezzogiorno in New York; Mario Mariotti, the inspiring artist and designer of the Mezzaluna logo and coordinator of all the art at Mezzaluna; Roberto Magris, dearest friend and architect who greatly influenced the design and look of Mezzaluna; Ralph J. Galasso, dear friend and lawyer, who was significant in making Mezzaluna a reality; Francesco Antonucci, owner of Remi in New York and a great friend and talented chef who encouraged and advised me during my work; Vladimir A. Lennox, a gifted photographer and artist; Pam Krauss, our very helpful and encouraging editor; Alberto Vitale, who made this project possible; and all the artists whose work graces our restaurant and the pages of this book.

Contents

Introduction

*L*IGHTS, CAMERA, PASTA, PIZZA, ACTION! It's no wonder Mezzaluna has been described as a Fellini movie: crowded, lively, and sexy. Such a vision of a contemporary Italian regional trattoria in New York, bursting with style and energy, had been dancing in my mind long before Mezzaluna's opening in 1984. As a transplanted Italian at the helm of Alfa Romeo USA with a lifelong passion for food, I longed for a place where I could meet with friends and enjoy some authentic Italian cuisine served in a casual, often chaotic, always amusing atmosphere. These are characteristics of trattorias in my native Milano. So, you can say that my switch from racy cars to zesty food came about from a personal need and the timely recognition that I was not alone in my quest for such a restaurant. Americans, who are great world travelers, had been exposed to Italy's incredibly rich culinary heritage and often wondered why they could not find the delicious regional dishes and succulent ingredients they had encountered during their journeys once they had returned home.

Mezzaluna, therefore, was born of a very clear goal: to offer a menu and an image of Italian cuisine that was very different from then-existing traditional Italian-American restaurants, using only the best ingredients. Fun, quick, daring, sophisticated, light, genuine, stimulating are all adjectives that reflect Mezzaluna's founding philosophy. I like to believe we began a gastronomic revolution when we were the first to place a bottle of extra-virgin olive oil as a standard condiment on every table. Olive oil is the king of our cuisine and probably the key to the success of the Mezzaluna formula. It was almost magical how quickly our customers became addicted to this new seasoning. From the very beginning, practically all the dishes on the menu had this one ingredient in common. We drizzle it on everything, from appetizers, salads, and carpaccios to soups, pasta, and pizza. At Mezzaluna, we import our own extra-virgin unfiltered olive oil from a small producer in Tuscany. We get a shipment of their new crop every January, which is very important, as olive oil has a shelf life of about only one year.

One of Mezzaluna's most innovative and lasting contributions is the menu's contemporary and informal structure; I like to call it Italian cuisine in blue jeans. It offers no "entrées" and relies solely on a good selection of appetizers, salads, carpaccios, pastas, and individual pizzas baked in a traditional brick wood-fired oven. The size of a dinner plate, the pizzas have a thin, slightly puffy crust with crisp brown edges and eclectic toppings and are irresistible. The common denominator for all of our recipes is simplicity, informality, and the use of high-quality, fresh, authentic ingredients. This is very much reflected in our seasonal pastas, which are the backbone of the Mezzaluna operations. Cooking seasonally means being able to take advantage of produce when it is at its peak, when the flavors and aromas are richest. Thanks to the versatility of pasta it is possible to create wonderful dishes year-round. We serve a wide variety of dried and fresh pastas, and every day among our specials we offer a seasonal stuffed pasta. For those with a yen for meat, we have created the hot carpaccios, which have become very popular and are wonderfully complemented by our salads. The grand finale and our signature dish is a dessert we introduced in 1984 and helped to popularize—the celebrated tiramisù. Like most of our desserts, it is eaten with a spoon, and according to a large throng of devotees it is still the best tiramisù around.

The world of Mezzaluna thrives under the delicate powder blue sky and fluffy clouds painted on the ceiling. There, we have tried to create an environment that blends the art of food, the love of art, and the Italian joy of living. It was an ensemble effort that included the talents of our architect, Roberto Magris, and graphic artist, Mario Mariotti, who designed our Mezzaluna logo, recalling both the half moon and the Mediterranean chopping tool. We also commissioned seventy-seven well-known Florentine artists to contribute their interpretations of the *mezzaluna*. Their paintings and collages form a whimsical mosaic that is permanently displayed at our restaurant.

In our commitment to authenticity, all the decor has been imported from Italy: the apricot marble tabletops, the high-backed folding Bonacina chairs, the Ginori china, Alessi flatware, and glassware by Bormioli. The floors are of the same terra-cotta tile as Brunelleschi's dome on the cathedral in Florence. The small bar is a late-nineteenth-century fabric display counter, and a Tuscan credenza from the 1700s is used to store Italian pottery, antique mezzalunas, old scales, and cookie jars.

The Mezzaluna world, I am happy to say, has expanded to the shores of the Bosporus. In Istanbul, amid minarets and exotic Turkish bazaars, our famed tiramisù may well conquer the traditional baklava. Closer to home, there are Mezzalunas in Aspen, Colorado, Brentwood and Corona del Mar in California, and most recently in Miami, Florida. It has been quite an adventure, and now, through these recipes, one you will be able to re-create in your own home.

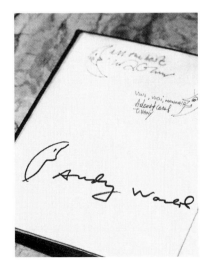

The Mezzaluna Pantry

*I*F ONE SINGLE FACTOR can be credited with the success of the Mezza-luna restaurants it is unquestionably our insistence on using only top-quality, authentic ingredients in our recipes. It may cost a bit more to use imported Italian pastas rather than domestic products, and it may require some detective work to search out a local source for delicacies like bottarga or caciotta cheese, but when you are making dishes as straightforward and simple as those we feature on our menus, any compromise in the ingredients will become apparent immediately. While I have suggested alternates and substitutions as well as mail-order sources (page 157) for some of the more unusual ingredients, for others no substitutions are possible. If, for instance, you cannot procure cotechino sausage for the sausage and lentil dish on page 13, move on to another recipe.

However, to cook in the style of Mezzaluna does not require an extensive list of esoteric ingredients, and most will be readily available at any well-stocked gourmet grocery, supplemented with fresh seasonal fruits and vegetables.

The pantry lists below describe some of the more unusual items called for in the recipes that follow as well as the specific varieties of such foods as capers, olives, and sun-dried tomatoes that give our dishes an unmistakably Italian flair.

HERBS AND SEASONINGS

Basil, chives, dill, Italian (flat-leaf, never curly) *parsley, mint, oregano, rosemary, sage, tarragon,* and *thyme* are the fresh herbs most often called for; *bay leaves* and *marjoram* are just about the only dried herbs we use. Supplement these with *dried saffron, black* and *white peppercorns* to be ground as needed, and *fine sea salt,* which has a mild, clean saline taste that does not overpower food. When dried hot pepper is called for, use *whole dried peppers* rather than bland red pepper flakes, and crumble them before measuring.

BEANS, NUTS, AND DRIED MUSHROOMS

Stock a selection of dried and/or canned beans, including: *canellini beans*—a very commonly used small bean that ranges from white to cream in color; *borlotti beans*—a somewhat larger bean that may have white stripes or vary from white to red to gray; *fava beans*—a large, meaty, pale green/gray bean that is also available fresh but is quite labor-consuming to prepare; *lentils*—preferably tiny dark brown Italian lentils or green lentils; *chick peas.*

Also keep on hand *pignoli (pine) nuts,* whose creamy kernels can turn rancid unless stored in the freezer, and *dry porcini mushrooms,* the most flavorful and costly of the Italian mushrooms, plus *dry shiitake mushrooms,* a less expensive alternative that can be used to stretch a small amount of porcinis.

CONDIMENTS

- *Oils,* including the finest quality *extra-virgin olive oil* you can afford; *corn oil* for deep frying; and *flavored oils,* such as *truffled oil* and *garlic oil,* for garnishes.
- *Vinegars,* including a good imported *red and white wine vinegar,* and a bottle of *balsamic vinegar,* the rich brown, aromatic vinegar that is aged from 3 to 10 years and is used to enhance flavors in finished dishes and salad dressings.
- *Brine-packed green* and *black olives,* preferably Ligurian or another small variety such as Niçoise or Gaeta.
- *Olive paste (olivada),* a flavorful, concentrated puree of black olives to stir into sauces, soups, or salad dressings.
- *Sun-dried tomatoes*—the Ligurian ones are the sweetest and softest, though any imported variety will do. Don't use the dry ones, as they can taste too bitter and strong once reconstituted.
- *Capers,* preferably Sicilian, preserved in salt. If you cannot locate Sicilian capers, choose small non-pareil capers in brine over the larger varieties.
- *Mostarda di Cremona,* a spicy chutney of whole candied fruits in a mustard seed syrup.

MEAT AND SEAFOOD

In addition to fresh provisions from the fish market and butcher, we keep the following on hand:

- *Canned Italian tuna* in olive oil.
- *Squid ink,* which comes fresh or frozen and is used to flavor sauces and color fresh pasta.

- *Bottarga,* the pressed roe of mullet (or, occasionally, tuna), which has been sun dried. To serve, shave pieces off with a vegetable peeler into pastas or over toasted country bread.
- *Anchovy fillets* packed in oil (the salt-packed fillets are simply too salty, even after rinsing).
- *Bresaola,* cured, air-dried, and seasoned beef that comes from the Valtellina area in northern Italy. *Viande de Grisons* (also known as *bunderfleisch*) is the Swiss counterpart and is widely available in gourmet stores.
- *Pancetta,* a leaner version of American bacon, is widely available from Italian delis and butchers. Regular slab bacon is an acceptable substitute.
- *Speck,* a pork specialty from Alto Adige, near Italy's border with Austria, is something like a smoked prosciutto, which can be used if speck is not available.
- *Prosciutto,* preferably the imported Parma variety.
- *Sausages,* including *cotechino,* a fresh pork sausage filled with a highly spiced, coarsely chopped mixture that can be found at Italian specialty butchers, and regular *sweet and spicy Italian sausage,* now readily available at supermarkets.

GRAINS AND FLOURS

- *Rice;* choose from among the many varieties based on the end use: *vialone nano* is a semifine, medium-grain rice, the best for risotto; *Carnaroli* is a superfine, long-grain rice that will work for risotto but is better suited to pilafs; *arborio,* another superfine, long-grain rice, is also a good choice for risottos.
- *Farro,* a soft-grain wheat, generally cooked in its unshelled state, has been used in Italy since ancient Rome and is today grown in central regions of Italy; *spelt* is the American counterpart.
- *Flours,* including 00 Italian flour, the high-protein, soft wheat flour that gives pizza dough its elasticity; durum semolina flour, for making pasta doughs.

CHEESE

In Italy more than 500 varieties of cheese exist in the various regions. The most common classification of Italian cheese is based on the time that elapses from production to readiness for consumption. *Fresh:* ready to be eaten immediately after production (mozzarella, caprino). *Soft:* ready after sixty days (taleggio, caciotta). *Semihard:* aged less than six months before consumption (fontina, asiago). *Hard:* aged over one year before consumption (parmigiano, provolone).

- *Parmesan,* imported varieties from the Parmigiano-Reggiano region only.
- *Grana padano,* similar to Parmesan but less expensive.
- *Mozzarella,* both fresh and smoked, and preferably handmade.
- *Pecorino* and peppered pecorino, hard cheese made with whole sheep's milk and with a strong taste. Typical of southern Italy.
- *Fresh ricotta,* for filling baked and stuffed pastas.
- *Ricotta salata,* a dry, aged cheese typical of southern Italy. Like Parmesan—but with a sharper tang—it can be grated over finished dishes; smoked ricotta salata, although less readily available, adds a mysterious, rich flavor to pasta.
- *Fresh goat cheese,* especially mild varieties such as caprini.
- *Mascarpone,* a rich, creamy fresh cheese that is integral to tiramisù.
- *Fontina,* the Italian melting cheese of choice, a regional specialty of Valle d'Aosta.
- *Asiago,* another mild, semi-hard cheese for grating into soups or over pasta.
- *Gorgonzola,* a creamy, strongly flavored blue cheese that pairs wonderfully with fruit and salad greens as well as creamy sauces. It should be used sparingly because of its richness.
- *Tuscan caciotta* or any other mild, semisoft sheep's milk cheese.
- *Caciocavallo,* originally from southern Italy, is compact and yellowish with a thin yellow crust. It is sweet when aged only two months and spicy when aged longer.
- *Provolone* can be sweet with a mild flavor when aged about one month, or *piccante* (spicy) when aged up to one year—the classic one to be used grated over pasta.
- *Stracchino* or *crescenza,* a soft and high-fat cheese made from whole milk, typical of the Lombardy region.

Appetizers

*A*PPETIZERS, along with pastas and pizzas, form the core of the menu at Mezzaluna, small but intensely flavored portions that excite the palate without filling the stomach. The American concept of the appetizer is unknown in Italy, where an antipasto plate or a small portion of pasta is the common prelude to a substantial main course of meat or fish. But in keeping with my aim of creating a lighter, more casual way of eating at the restaurant, I had the notion of introducing smaller portions of regional Italian dishes at the start of the meal, not unlike an Italian version of tapas, the popular tidbits served in Spanish taverns. The appetizers we serve at Mezzaluna are light, amusing, and colorful, either as a tempting taste before a dish of pasta or a pizza, or in combinations of two or more and accompanied perhaps by a salad, as a satisfying meal on their own. An array of these appetizers, along with a baked pasta, would make a wonderful party buffet.

Polenta alla griglia con ragù di funghi e fontina

GRILLED POLENTA WITH RAGOUT OF WILD MUSHROOMS AND FONTINA

*Polenta is a yellow cornmeal that has been cooked with water and seasonings.
In the 1700s it was served as a side dish with stewed meat leftovers or as a main
meal with some butter and cheese. Thanks to the gastronomic movement to revive
regional cuisine, this "fare of the poor" has made a resounding comeback.*

1 quart cold water

1 cup yellow cornmeal

Fine sea salt to taste

1 tablespoon unsalted butter

½ cup dry porcini mushrooms

5 tablespoons extra-virgin
olive oil

2 garlic cloves

½ pound fresh shiitake
mushrooms, quartered

¼ pound fresh chanterelle
mushrooms, cut in 2-inch slices

¼ pound oyster mushrooms,
cut in 2-inch slices

8 slices fontina cheese

2 tablespoons chopped fresh
Italian parsley

1. In a casserole, bring the water to a boil. With your hand, gradually sift in the cornmeal. Cook for 10 minutes, stirring constantly, until thick. Season with salt and stir in the butter. Spread the polenta onto a large baking sheet and allow it to cool. Cut diagonally into diamond shapes. On a stovetop grill, grill the polenta diamonds on both sides.

2. In a saucepan, combine the porcini mushrooms with 2 cups water. Bring to a boil and cook for 3 minutes, until they become soft. Drain and pat dry.

3. In a heavy skillet, heat the olive oil and sauté the garlic until lightly golden. Add the porcini, shiitake, chanterelle, and oyster mushrooms and cook over low heat for 15 minutes, until very soft. Keep warm.

4. Preheat the broiler.

5. Place the grilled polenta in a baking dish. Cover each polenta diamond with slices of fontina cheese. Broil briefly, until the cheese has melted.

6. Arrange the polenta-fontina diamonds on individual plates, top with a dollop of piping hot mushroom *ragù*, and garnish with the parsley.

SERVES 4 TO 6

Bocconcini di mozzarella, peperoni arrostiti, pomodori, e basilico

FRESH MOZZARELLA WITH ROASTED PEPPERS, TOMATOES, AND BASIL

At the time when I first opened Mezzaluna it was difficult to find fresh mozzarella every day in New York, so I decided to enlist the services of fourth-generation master mozzarella maker Giuseppe Cuomo, also known as "Joe Mozzarella." A native of Vico Equense near Naples, Joe makes the mozzarella right on our premises like in the old days. In the summer and fall we combine it with roasted peppers and fresh beefsteak tomatoes. In the winter, we use oven-roasted tomatoes (page 110) instead; the roasting process brings up all the flavors and aromas of summer. And while you're roasting peppers, make a few extra to marinate (recipe follows).

2 yellow bell peppers	Fine sea salt and freshly ground black pepper
2 red bell peppers	
2 ripe beefsteak tomatoes	Extra-virgin olive oil
8 fresh mozzarella *bocconcini* (about 2 ounces each), halved	2 tablespoons chopped fresh basil

1. Preheat the oven to 450° F. Place the whole peppers on a baking sheet and roast until the skins begin to char and blister. Turn often to avoid burning and so they roast evenly. Remove from the oven, place in a bowl, and cover with plastic wrap for ½ hour. Peel the peppers and remove the stems. Quarter the peppers and remove the ribs and seeds. Set aside.

2. Slice the tomatoes. Arrange 4 *bocconcini* halves in the center of each individual plate. Arrange alternating slices of tomato and roasted peppers around the *bocconcini*. Season with salt and pepper, drizzle with olive oil, and garnish generously with fresh basil.

SERVES 4

6 red or yellow peppers, roasted, peeled, and seeded	**Fine sea salt and freshly ground white pepper**
4 garlic cloves, thinly sliced	**2 cups extra-virgin olive oil**
Fresh basil leaves	

In a terrine, combine layers of peppers with sliced garlic and basil leaves and season with salt and pepper. Add the olive oil. Marinate covered with plastic wrap for at least 24 hours in the refrigerator. Do not marinate for more than 3 days. Remove from the refrigerator at least an hour before serving.

Carabiniere a cavallo

GRILLED SMOKED MOZZARELLA, RADICCHIO, AND PANCETTA

This dish translates as "mounted policeman," so named because the color and the fan shape of the radicchio reminded me of a carabiniere's hat.

2 medium heads radicchio, halved	**4 thick slices smoked mozzarella cheese (*scamorza*)**
1 tablespoon extra-virgin olive oil	**Fine sea salt and freshly ground white pepper**
8 slices pancetta or slab bacon	

1. Rinse the radicchio and pat it dry. Cut in quarters. Do not trim the stem, as it helps hold the leaves together.

2. Preheat a stovetop nonstick grill pan for 3 minutes. Brush the radicchio with olive oil and place on the grill. Add the pancetta slices and grill together for about 3 minutes on each side, or until the radicchio is tender. (This allows the radicchio to absorb the smoked aroma of the pancetta.)

3. Raise the grill's temperature to its maximum. Grill the smoked mozzarella slices briefly, just until grill marks appear on the surface.

4. On individual plates, fan 2 of the radicchio quarters. Top with 2 pancetta slices and a slice of grilled cheese. Drizzle with olive oil and season with salt and pepper to taste.

SERVES 4

Grigliata mista di verdure con olio tartufato

MIXED GRILLED VEGETABLES WITH TRUFFLED OIL

*The secret of this recipe is that the vegetables are cut almost paper thin, which
makes them more digestible. This also helps the moisture cook off more quickly
and makes grilling easier. It is a wonderful vegetarian dish and a lunchtime favorite
at Mezzaluna. A sprinkle of truffled oil enhances the flavor of the vegetables, but
garlic-infused olive oil is a pleasant substitute if truffled oil is unavailable.*

1 medium eggplant	2 zucchini
1 fennel bulb	3 tablespoons extra-virgin olive oil
1 red bell pepper	
1 yellow bell pepper	Fine sea salt and freshly ground black pepper
2 Belgian endives	
8 shiitake mushrooms, stems discarded	Chopped fresh basil
	1 tablespoon truffled olive oil or garlic olive oil (see Note, page 10)
1 large beefsteak tomato	

1. Trim the eggplant, slice thinly, and arrange the slices in a colander. Sprinkle
with salt and set aside until it releases its liquid.

2. In the meantime, prepare the rest of the vegetables. Rinse the fennel and
remove the outer layer until you get to the core. Cut the core into ¼-inch slices.
Rinse, trim and seed the peppers, and slice into quarters. Halve the Belgian
endives. Brush the mushroom caps and wipe with a damp paper towel. Quarter
the tomato. Rinse and trim the zucchini, then cut on the diagonal into thin slices.

3. When the eggplant has released its moisture, rinse the slices briefly
and pat dry.

4. Heat a grill pan and brush it with olive oil. Grill all the vegetables in batches
for 2 to 3 minutes on each side, until browned and tender. Season with salt and
pepper to taste.

5. Arrange the vegetables on a platter. Garnish with basil and drizzle with the
truffled olive oil.

SERVES 4

Bresaola con finocchi in salsa piccante

SUN-DRIED CURED BEEF WITH FENNEL IN SPICY SAUCE

This dish derives its unique flavor and texture from bresaola, *a dark red cured dried beef similar to the Swiss* viande de Grisons. *Particular to the Valtellina region, it is generally made from beef fillet treated with a mixture of salt and spices, then wrapped in thin nets and aged for at least one month. The* bresaola, *from the word* brasare, *meaning "braise," is marinated in wine and aromatic herbs. (See The Mezzaluna Pantry on page xii for more information.)*

½ pound *bresaola* or *viande de Grisons*

2 medium fennel bulbs

2 tablespoons extra-virgin olive oil

Juice of ½ lemon

1 teaspoon Dijon mustard

Fine sea salt and freshly ground black pepper

½ teaspoon cayenne pepper

1. Cut the *bresaola* paper thin and arrange on individual dishes, about 8 slices per serving, to cover each plate.

2. Discard the tough outer layers of the fennel and cut the inner core in julienne strips. Mound in the center of each serving.

3. In a bowl, combine the olive oil, lemon juice, mustard, salt, pepper, and cayenne pepper. Whisk vigorously until smooth.

4. Pour the dressing over the *bresaola* and fennel and serve.

SERVES 4

Vitello tonnato

SLICED COLD VEAL IN TUNA SAUCE

Vitello tonnato originated in Lombardy, in the Milano area. Ours is
an expedient and accessible rendition of this otherwise complicated dish,
which in its original version does not use mayonnaise; that addition came
from the Piedmontese, under the influence of their French neighbors.

2 pounds veal tenderloin	3 cups water
1 tablespoon extra-virgin olive oil	1 6-ounce can tuna in olive oil, drained
2 cups dry white wine	
1 onion, chopped	4 Italian anchovy fillets, packed in olive oil, drained
1 carrot, peeled and sliced	
1 celery stalk, chopped	2 tablespoons Sicilian capers, preserved in salt
4 bay leaves	Juice of 1 lemon
Fine sea salt and freshly ground black pepper	1 cup mayonnaise
	1 lemon, sliced, for garnish

1. In a large casserole, brown the veal well on all sides in the olive oil. Add the wine, onion, carrot, celery, bay leaves, salt and pepper, and water. Cover, bring to a boil, and simmer over medium heat for 1 hour.

2. Remove the meat from the liquid and let it cool.

3. Strain the cooking liquid into a saucepan. Bring to a boil over high heat and cook until the liquid has reduced by half. Set aside to cool.

4. In a food processor, combine the drained tuna, the anchovies, two-thirds of the capers, 3 tablespoons of the cooled cooking liquid, the lemon juice, and the mayonnaise. Process until the sauce is smooth and creamy. If it is too thick, thin it with olive oil or white wine.

5. Slice the veal thinly. Arrange 2 or 3 slices on individual plates and garnish with the remaining capers and lemon slices. Pass the sauce separately.

SERVES 4

Tartare di salmone fresco alle tre erbe

Three separate tartares with three very distinctive flavors is what sets this recipe apart. The idea came to me in France where I sampled a marinated salmon tartare prepared with six different herbs. I have selected tarragon, basil, and chives because they are especially flavorful and well suited to the salmon.

1 pound very fresh salmon fillet

3 tablespoons extra-virgin olive oil

3 tablespoons fresh lemon juice

¼ cup very finely chopped chives

¼ cup very finely chopped fresh tarragon leaves

10 fresh basil leaves, very finely chopped

Freshly ground white pepper

Fresh basil leaves, for garnish

1 plum tomato, finely diced, for garnish

1. With a sharp knife, chop the salmon fillet into very fine pieces. Divide into 3 equal portions and place each in a separate bowl. Add 1 tablespoon olive oil and 1 tablespoon lemon juice to each portion. Add the chives to one bowl, the tarragon to the second, and the basil to the third. With your hands, mix the ingredients in each terrine until well combined. Season all 3 with pepper and mix well. Marinate for 15 minutes.

2. Using a spoon, shape the contents of each bowl into 4 to 6 oval mounds. On individual plates, arrange a salmon-tarragon, salmon-chive, and salmon-basil mound in the shape of a 3-pointed star. Decorate the center with a sprig of basil and sprinkle some finely diced tomato all around.

SERVES 4 TO 6

Gamberetti e fagioli alla Veneziana

SHRIMP AND WHITE BEANS, VENETIAN STYLE

This is a wonderful appetizer for both summer and winter,
one I have often enjoyed at sunset in Venice with a cold glass of sparkling
Prosecco. The addition of olive oil at the last moment enhances and seals the
flavors. In colder months, serve this dish warm by sautéing the shrimp
for 2 or 3 minutes in rosemary-flavored olive oil (see Note).

1½ cups dry white beans (cannellini)

Fine sea salt and freshly ground black pepper

Mezzaluna herb bouquet (2 sprigs of fresh rosemary, 2 bay leaves, 3 sprigs of thyme, 3 sprigs of parsley)

4 garlic cloves, unpeeled

1 pound medium shrimp (about 36)

2 celery stalks, chopped

Juice of 1 lemon

2 tablespoons chopped fresh Italian parsley

⅓ cup extra-virgin olive oil

1. Soak the cannellini beans in cold water for 12 hours or overnight. The following day, drain the beans and transfer them to a large pot of lightly salted cold water. Add the Mezzaluna herb bouquet and the unpeeled garlic cloves. Bring to a boil, then reduce the heat and cook for 1½ hours, or until the beans are tender. Drain and discard the herb bouquet and garlic.

2. Cook the shrimp in boiling salted water for 2 minutes. Immediately drain, shell and devein, and place in a mixing bowl with the beans.

3. Add the celery to the shrimp and beans. Add the lemon juice and chopped parsley. Season with salt and pepper, toss well, and add the olive oil. Toss again and serve at room temperature.

SERVES 4

NOTE: To make your own rosemary-flavored oil, in a clean jar, mix ⅓ cup minced rosemary (use a *mezzaluna* or sharp knife to chop the rosemary leaves) with 1 cup extra-virgin olive oil and shake well. Let sit at room temperature for 2 hours, then refrigerate for 3 days before using. Strain the oil and store up to 2 or 3 weeks in the refrigerator. For garlic oil, replace the rosemary with 1 tablespoon of chopped fresh garlic. Let stand at room temperature for 15 minutes, then refrigerate and strain as above.

Calamari saltati con pomodoro, avocado, e peperoncino

CALAMARI SAUTÉED WITH TOMATO, AVOCADO, AND FRESH CHILI PEPPER

A top seller at our restaurant for many years, this is an adaptation of a recipe prepared by my friend Sandro Fioriti, a talented and versatile chef who featured it at his restaurant, Sandro's, where I first had the opportunity to taste it.

POACHING LIQUID
1 quart cold water
1 tablespoon vinegar
Sea salt to taste
1 carrot, peeled
1 onion
1 celery stalk
2 bay leaves

¼ pound calamari, sliced into ¼-inch rings

1 garlic clove, chopped
4 tablespoons extra-virgin olive oil
1 beefsteak tomato, peeled, seeded, and diced
1 avocado (not too ripe), diced
1 teaspoon chopped fresh chili pepper
2 bunches *frisée* lettuce, separated into small pieces
2 tablespoons chopped fresh Italian parsley
Fine sea salt and freshly ground black pepper

1. In a large pot, combine all the ingredients for the poaching liquid. Cover the pot and bring to a boil. When the water is boiling, add the sliced calamari and cook just until it turns white, 2 or 3 minutes. Drain well and set aside. Do not overcook the calamari as it will become rubbery.

2. In a skillet, sauté the garlic in the olive oil until fragrant, a minute or two. Add the tomato, avocado, and chili pepper and sauté for a few minutes just to heat through.

3. Add the calamari rings and *frisée* and sauté for 1 minute, blending all the ingredients. Sprinkle with parsley and a drizzle of olive oil. Season with salt and pepper to taste and serve immediately.

SERVES 4

Lenticchie con salsiccia piccante alla griglia e Mostarda di Cremona

WARM LENTILS WITH SPICY GRILLED SAUSAGE AND
WHOLE CANDIED FRUITS IN MUSTARD SYRUP

This is a perfect New Year's Eve dish, as lentils are believed to bring money when eaten at the beginning of the year. Mostarda di Cremona, *a candied fruit chutney in mustard syrup, is available in Italian specialty stores.*

1 pound dried Italian or green lentils	2 cups beef broth
2 tablespoons extra-virgin olive oil	Mezzaluna herb bouquet (2 sprigs of fresh rosemary, 2 bay leaves, 3 sprigs of thyme, 3 sprigs of parsley)
1 onion, chopped	
1 carrot, peeled and diced	
1 celery stalk, chopped	6 spicy fresh Italian sausages
4 ounces pancetta or slab bacon, diced	6 tablespoons *Mostarda di Cremona* or other mixed fruit chutney with mustard seeds, coarsely chopped

1. Soak the lentils overnight in cold water to cover by 1 inch.

2. The next day, heat the olive oil in a casserole. Sauté the onion over medium heat until lightly golden. Add the carrot, celery, and diced pancetta and cook for a few minutes until golden brown. Drain the lentils, add to the skillet, and sauté for 2 minutes. Add 2 cups water, the beef broth, and the herb bouquet; cover and bring to a boil. Lower the flame to medium and cook for about 1½ hours, or until the lentils are tender, adding more water if necessary.

3. Heat a stovetop grill pan or preheat the broiler. Butterfly the sausages and grill or broil on both sides until browned and crisp.

4. Divide the lentils among 6 individual plates and top with a grilled sausage and 1 tablespoon of the candied fruit in its syrup.

SERVES 6

Totani in zimino

*This Ligurian dish, which found its way to Tuscany, can be served with a side
dish of steamed rice. It is said to be of Arab origin; the words* in zimino *come from
the Arab word* samin. *Through the centuries, it has come to signify a method
of cooking fish in butter or olive oil and a sauce of green vegetables.*

1 pound cuttlefish or the smallest calamari available	**½ cup dry white wine**
½ cup extra-virgin olive oil	**4–5 ripe plum tomatoes, chopped**
1 garlic clove, minced	**2 pounds Swiss chard or spinach**
½ medium onion, chopped	**1 whole garlic clove**
1 celery stalk, finely minced	**1 teaspoon chopped fresh chili pepper**
½ cup minced leek	**2 tablespoons chopped fresh Italian parsley**
Fine sea salt and freshly ground black pepper	

1. Clean the cuttlefish, removing the black skin, eyes, mouth, ink sac, and interior (see Note). Wash and rinse thoroughly. Cut the tentacles in small pieces and the rest in thin strips about ¼ inch wide.

2. In a heavy skillet, heat 4 tablespoons of olive oil over medium heat. Add the minced garlic and sauté until lightly golden, a minute or two. Add the onion, celery, and leek and cook until tender but not brown, 6 to 8 minutes. Add the cuttlefish, season with salt and pepper, and sauté for 3 minutes. Add the white wine and cook over medium-high heat until it evaporates. Add the chopped tomatoes, cover, and continue to cook over medium heat for 40 minutes, or until the cuttlefish is tender. (If using calamari, reduce the cooking time to 25 to 30 minutes.)

3. Wash and rinse the Swiss chard. Blanch in a large pot of boiling water for 1 minute. Drain and chop coarsely. Place in a skillet with the water still clinging to the leaves; cover and steam over high heat for 3 to 4 minutes, turning often. Wipe out the skillet and add the remaining 4 tablespoons of olive oil. Add the Swiss chard, whole garlic clove, and chopped chili pepper and sauté over medium heat for 5 minutes. Season with salt and pepper to taste.

4. Stir the Swiss chard into the cuttlefish and continue to cook for an additional 10 to 15 minutes, or until any excess liquid has evaporated. Adjust the seasonings and sprinkle with parsley.

SERVES 4

NOTE: To remove the ink sacs more easily, place the cuttlefish in the freezer for 30 minutes, or until the ink sac has frozen. It can then be removed with your fingers.

Carne cruda all'Albese

VEAL TARTARE, PIEDMONT STYLE

An ancestor of carpaccio, this is a centuries-old dish. It was usually made with thinly cut veal slices that were marinated in lemon or chopped à la tartare. To reduce the possibility of contamination, do not use ground meat from the butcher; instead, chop it by hand yourself. In order to preserve the color and freshness of the meat, wait until the last minute to mix in the lemon juice. When available, you may top the veal with truffle or fresh porcini mushroom shavings.

1 pound veal tenderloin	1½ teaspoons very finely chopped fresh Italian parsley
5 tablespoons extra-virgin olive oil	
1 garlic clove, pressed	Juice of 2 lemons
1 teaspoon truffle paste	Fine sea salt and freshly ground black pepper

1. On a cutting board, with a sharp butcher knife, chop the veal into very fine pieces. Do not use the food processor for this, as the texture will be too soft.
2. Place the meat in a mixing bowl with the olive oil, garlic, truffle paste, and parsley. Mix well, cover, and marinate for about 30 minutes in the refrigerator.
3. Just before serving, add the lemon juice and season with salt and pepper. Arrange in small mounds on individual plates.

SERVES 4

TIP: A "magic" way to rid your fingers of garlic odor is to make contact with the knife blade as you rinse it under cold water. For better-tasting garlic, cut the clove in half and remove the green "stem."

Risotto giallo alla Milanese

SAFFRON RISOTTO

This is a luscious side dish that is even better prepared ahead and used as the basis for stuffed rice croquettes, or formed into cakes and sautéed (see page 19). The quantities below should yield 4 generous appetizer servings with enough left over for 1 large risotto cake.

SAFFRON STOCK	¼ cup extra-virgin olive oil
3 quarts water	½ medium onion, chopped
1 carrot	3 cups Italian rice, preferably carnaroli, vialone nano, or arborio
2 celery stalks	
2 onions	½ cup white wine
1 bunch parsley	Fine sea salt and freshly ground black pepper to taste
1 bunch scallions	
Fine sea salt	¼ cup (4 tablespoons) unsalted butter
1 teaspoon saffron threads	⅓ cup grated Parmesan cheese

1. To make the stock, combine the water, carrot, celery, onions, parsley, and scallions in a stockpot. Bring to a boil, then reduce the heat and simmer for 1 hour. Strain the broth, discarding the vegetables. Return the stock to the pot, return to a boil, and season with salt and the saffron. Set aside.

2. In a heavy casserole, heat the olive oil. Add the chopped onion and cook until lightly golden. Add the rice, stirring for 2 to 3 minutes until it is well coated.

3. Add the white wine and allow it to evaporate. Add 1 cup of the hot saffron stock and continue to cook over high heat for 15 minutes, stirring constantly, and adding more of the saffron stock as the liquid is absorbed; you will use approximately 5 to 6 cups in all. The rice should be creamy but still firm to the bite, or al dente.

4. Season with salt and pepper. Add the butter and grated Parmesan cheese and mix well.

SERVES 6 TO 8

Arancini di riso solari

STUFFED YELLOW (SAFFRON) RICE CROQUETTES

This is my take on the traditional arancini di riso *recipe, a popular finger food of southern Italy. As a Milanese, I have substituted saffron risotto for the more usual boiled rice, as it is creamier and more flavorful. Use any leftover risotto you may have.*

CROQUETTE STUFFING

1 garlic clove, chopped

½ onion, chopped

1 celery stalk, chopped

3 tablespoons extra-virgin olive oil

⅓ pound ground veal

½ cup dry white wine

2 tablespoons tomato paste diluted in 1 cup water

1 ounce dried porcini mushrooms (soaked in warm water for 15 minutes and drained), diced

Fine sea salt and freshly ground black pepper

⅓ cup steamed peas

4 ounces fresh mozzarella cheese, cubed

1 tablespoon chopped fresh basil

Cooled *Risotto giallo alla Milanese* (page 16)

3 tablespoons flour

3 eggs, beaten

⅓ cup bread crumbs

5 tablespoons extra-virgin olive oil

½ cup warm Mezzaluna Tomato Sauce (page 73)

1. In a saucepan, sauté the garlic, onion, and celery in 3 tablespoons olive oil. Add the ground veal and cook over medium heat for 5 to 7 minutes, breaking up with a wooden spoon, until golden brown. Add the wine and cook until it evaporates. Add the diluted tomato paste, cover, and cook over low heat for at least 2 hours, adding water if necessary. Add the porcini mushrooms and cook for an additional 20 minutes; the liquid should be quite reduced. Season with salt and pepper to taste.

2. In a bowl, mix the peas with the cubed mozzarella and fresh basil. Set aside.

3. With your hands, mold the rice into small spheres about the size of a tangerine. Cut the spheres in half. With a teaspoon, scoop a well in the center of each half. Fill one half with some of the meat ragu and the other half with the mozzarella-pea mixture. Press the 2 halves together again and roll in the flour. Dredge the croquettes in the beaten egg and then in the bread crumbs.

4. Heat 5 tablespoons olive oil in a skillet until very hot. Add the croquettes and sauté until they are golden brown. Drain on a paper towel and allow to cool. Just-before serving, preheat the oven to 350°F. Place the rice croquettes in a baking pan and bake for 5 minutes, until the crust becomes crispy.

5. Cover individual dishes with 2 tablespoons of Mezzaluna Tomato Sauce. Arrange the croquettes on top of the sauce.

SERVES 4 TO 6

Risotto al salto

SAUTÉED RISOTTO CAKES

3 tablespoons unsalted butter	**¼ cup grated Parmesan cheese,**
1½ cups leftover risotto	**plus more for serving**
	Freshly ground black pepper

In a nonstick skillet, melt the butter until lightly golden. Add the risotto to the skillet and flatten with a spoon or fork into a ¼-inch-thick pancake. Sauté for 3 to 4 minutes until a golden crust has formed. Sprinkle the top with the grated Parmesan cheese. Flip the pancake over with the help of a spatula and sauté for 3 to 4 minutes on the second side, cut into wedges, and serve with grated Parmesan cheese and freshly ground pepper.

SERVES 2

Soups

*A*MONG THE PEASANT COOK'S most important contributions to Italian cuisine is a vast and diverse legacy of soup cookery. For centuries soup was the centerpiece of most peasant meals, one that challenged their resourcefulness and inventiveness every day, resulting in hundreds of interesting and unusual variations. Our menu offers a small selection, about twelve in all, which we rotate according to the seasons and what fresh produce is available. An all-time favorite is our special take on *pasta e fagioli*, a succulent southern Italian version with clams. According to some food historians, *pasta e fagioli* is the common denominator of all Italian regional cuisines and might in fact be considered the national dish; certainly the combination of beans and pasta with vegetables is found in every region of Italy. Other offerings from our historical soup mosaic include a vegetable minestrone from northern Italy, the *Gran Farro,* which fed the Roman legions, and the amusing *Le Virtù,* a spring ritual that ensures prosperity. Served with a bracing glass of red wine and perhaps a fresh focaccia (plain or stuffed), and always garnished with a C-shaped swirl of extra-virgin olive oil, this is intensely satisfying fare that belies its humble origins.

Pasta e fagioli con le vongole

PASTA AND BEANS WITH CLAMS

In southern Italy, this classic soup is prepared with assorted dry pasta as
well as with peperoncini peppers, which gives it a delightful piquancy.

14 ounces dry cannellini beans,
soaked overnight and drained

Mezzaluna herb bouquet (2 sprigs
of fresh rosemary, 2 bay leaves, 3
sprigs of thyme, 3 sprigs of parsley)

6 tablespoons extra-virgin olive oil

1 garlic clove, chopped

½ celery stalk, chopped

½ carrot, chopped

1 medium onion, chopped

1 sprig of rosemary, chopped

4 fresh sage leaves, chopped

1 teaspoon chopped
fresh chili pepper

4 ripe plum tomatoes, chopped

2 cups Saffron Stock (page 16)

CLAM SAUCE

4 tablespoons extra-virgin olive oil

1 garlic clove, chopped

24 Manilla clams

2 tablespoons chopped
fresh Italian parsley

½ teaspoon chopped chili pepper

½ pound assorted dry pasta

Fine sea salt and freshly ground
black pepper to taste

1. Stir the cannellini beans into a large pot with cold salted water to cover. Add
the Mezzaluna herb bouquet. Bring to a boil, lower the flame, and simmer until
the beans are soft, about 1½ hours. Drain and discard the herb bouquet.

2. In a saucepan, heat 6 tablespoons of oil. Add them the chopped garlic, celery,
carrot, onion, rosemary, sage leaves, and chili pepper. Cook until lightly golden.
Add the chopped tomato. Cover and simmer for 30 minutes on a low flame.

3. Puree half the beans in a food processor. Add to the vegetables. Add the
remaining beans and the stock and simmer for an additional 10 minutes.

4. In a skillet, heat 4 tablespoons of olive oil. Add the garlic and clams and cook
on a high flame until the clams open. Sprinkle with the parsley and chili pepper.
Shuck the clams and strain their cooking liquid. Add both to the soup and cook
for 3 to 5 minutes. Add the pasta and cook until it is tender.

5. Ladle the soup into individual dishes, add a dash of olive oil, and season.

SERVES 4 TO 6

Pappa col pomodoro

*This is a classical Tuscan recipe. Every trattoria has its own version.
It was an old belief that eating this soup would enhance your looks, a legend that
probably traces back to eager mothers coaxing their children to consume this healthy
dish with a special appetite. Our* pappa col pomodoro *replaces the usual onion with a
leek to make it more digestible; the addition of rosemary gives it a special aroma.*

Extra-virgin olive oil

1 medium leek, finely chopped

2 garlic cloves, chopped

1 teaspoon chopped fresh chili pepper

½ pound stale Tuscan peasant bread, coarsely sliced (see Note)

8 ripe plum tomatoes

8 fresh basil leaves, chopped

3 sprigs fresh rosemary leaves, chopped

1 tablespoon tomato paste

1 quart beef broth

Fine sea salt and freshly ground black pepper

1. In a large saucepan, heat 6 tablespoons of olive oil. Add the leek, garlic, and chili pepper and sauté until lightly golden. Add the bread, tomatoes, basil, rosemary, and tomato paste, and cook over a medium flame for 5 minutes. Lower the flame, cover, and continue to cook for 1 hour, adding the beef broth gradually. The bread should be very soft and the mixture uniform. Add broth or water if you feel the consistency is too thick. Season with salt and pepper to taste and a drizzle of olive oil. Transfer the soup into a terra-cotta dish and allow it to rest for 1 hour at room temperature before serving.

2. Serve the soup hot, cold, at room temperature, or reheated. Always top with a C of olive oil and never add grated Parmesan cheese.

SERVES 4 TO 6

NOTE: The bread should be at least 2 days old. I prefer the texture to be on the dense side.

Minestrone di verdure con riso

VEGETABLE MINESTRONE WITH RICE

A typically northern Italian dish, minestrone *means big soup. The word refers both to the density of the soup as well as the use of a large number of ingredients. Minestrone traditionally contains one or more thickening vegetables (potatoes, beans, peas, or the like); pasta or rice; oil, lard, or pancetta depending on the region; and a variety of vegetables. Eaten hot, it is a hearty winter soup. It is also excellent at room temperature in the summer.*

5 tablespoons extra-virgin olive oil

1 medium onion, chopped

3½ ounces prosciutto, pancetta, or slab bacon, diced

1 garlic clove, chopped

2 leeks, chopped

2 carrots, chopped

3 celery stalks, chopped

3 zucchini, diced

1 potato, diced

1 cup cooked borlotti or cannellini beans

1 cup fresh or thawed frozen tiny green peas

2 bay leaves

4 sage leaves

1 cup crushed peeled tomatoes

1 cup arborio rice

Fine sea salt and freshly ground black pepper

1 tablespoon chopped fresh basil leaves

1 tablespoon chopped fresh Italian parsley

Grated Parmesan cheese

1. In a large saucepan, heat the olive oil. Add the onion and prosciutto and sauté until lightly golden. Add the garlic, leeks, carrots, and celery. Cook for 15 minutes on a medium flame. Add the zucchini, potato, beans, peas, bay leaves, sage, and tomatoes. Cook for 5 minutes. Add water to cover and cook on a low flame for 40 minutes. Add the rice and cook for an additional 18 minutes. Season with salt and pepper, sprinkle with basil and parsley, and ladle the soup into individual dishes.

2. Serve with a sprinkle of grated Parmesan cheese and a drop of olive oil.

SERVES 4 TO 6

Gran Farro

SPELT SOUP

Farro, a kind of soft-grain wheat also known as spelt, has a history and tradition going back to ancient Rome. The Latins used the farro *flour to make "puls," a sort of polenta, which became a basic staple in their diet. Although wheat displaced* farro *as the grain of choice during the Renaissance, today it is once again in fashion, and is grown in Umbria, Lazio, and Tuscany.*

1¼-pound mixture of borlotti and cannellini beans	10 fresh marjoram leaves, chopped
½ pound *farro* (spelt)	2 ounces prosciutto, cut in julienne
Extra-virgin olive oil	3 ripe plum tomatoes, chopped
1 small onion, chopped	Pinch of nutmeg
2 garlic cloves	Fine sea salt and freshly ground black pepper
1 celery stalk, chopped	
6 fresh sage leaves, chopped	

1. Stir the beans into a large pot filled with salted cold water to cover. Bring to a boil, lower the flame, and simmer until the beans are tender, about an hour. Drain, reserving the cooking liquid. Pass the beans through a food mill until you have obtained a puree.

2. Soak the spelt in cold water for a few minutes. Discard the soaking water and any impurities, drain, and pat dry.

3. In a casserole, heat 6 tablespoons of olive oil. Add the onion, garlic, celery, sage, and marjoram and sauté until lightly golden. Add the prosciutto and brown for 1 minute. Add the tomatoes and nutmeg and cook for 20 minutes over medium heat. Process the mixture in a food processor.

4. Transfer the mixture to a large pot and combine with the pureed beans, the spelt, and the reserved bean cooking liquid. Simmer over a low flame for 30 minutes, season with salt and pepper, then simmer for an additional 10 minutes.

5. Ladle the soup into individual dishes. Serve with a C of olive oil.

SERVES 6

Ribollita

THICK TUSCAN BREAD VEGETABLE SOUP

The origin of this famous soup, which is typical of Florentine fare, lies in the word ribollita, *meaning "reboiled." It was generally prepared with leftover vegetables and stale Tuscan bread. It was allowed to rest in a terra-cotta dish and heated slowly on a wood-burning stove for many hours. This procedure created a wonderful thick and velvety texture that greatly enhanced the flavor of the vegetables. It was often eaten for breakfast. Our recipe is a faithful rendition of the classic* ribollita, *except we have substituted savoy cabbage for the "black cabbage" of the Tuscan countryside, which is not often found in the United States.*

10½ ounces cannellini beans, soaked overnight and drained

3 whole garlic cloves

1 bay leaf

Extra-virgin olive oil

2 garlic cloves, chopped

2 medium onions, chopped

2 carrots, sliced

2 celery stalks with leaves, chopped

2 leeks, finely chopped

Herbs: 4 sprigs of parsley, 4 large basil leaves, 3 sage leaves, 3 sprigs of rosemary, 3 sprigs of thyme

1 tablespoon tomato paste dissolved in 1 cup warm water

4 ripe plum tomatoes, chopped

2 potatoes, quartered

1 head savoy cabbage

1 bunch Swiss chard, coarsely chopped

2 cups beef broth

1 loaf Tuscan bread, sliced

1 tablespoon chopped chives

Fine sea salt and freshly ground black pepper

1. Stir the beans into a large pot with cold salted water to cover. Add 2 whole garlic cloves and the bay leaf, bring to a boil, lower the flame, and simmer for 1½ hours, until the beans are soft. Drain and discard the seasonings.

2. In a large heavy skillet, heat 4 tablespoons of olive oil. Sauté the chopped garlic and onions until lightly golden. Add the carrots, celery, leeks, and herbs. Add the tomato paste, plum tomatoes, the potatoes, cabbage, and chard. Cook for about 5 to 10 minutes. Add the beef broth and half of the cannellini beans with their liquid passed through a food mill. If necessary, add some water to dilute the soup. Bring to a boil and simmer for 1 hour. Add the remaining whole cannellini beans and cook for a few minutes.

3. In a large terra-cotta terrine, alternate layers of the sliced Tuscan bread with layers of the soup. Make at least 3 layers. Drizzle with olive oil. Allow it to rest for a couple of hours, or until the next day.

4. Reheat the *ribollita* with chives and garlic: In a large pan, heat 2 tablespoons of olive oil. Sauté the remaining whole garlic clove with the chives until lightly golden. Discard the garlic after it is golden. Add the soup and heat for about 10 minutes over a medium flame. It has to have a thick consistency. Ladle the soup into individual dishes.

5. Serve with a C of olive oil, salt, and freshly ground pepper.

SERVES 6

Le Virtù

*A springtime tradition that celebrates prosperity, Le Virtù was prepared
with vegetables left over from winter preserves. The number of ingredients should
be equal to the virtues possessed by the "perfect mistress of the house."*

1 cup mixed dry beans
(dry chickpeas and dry lentils),
soaked overnight and drained

8 ounces fresh shelled fava beans

8 ounces fresh or thawed
frozen tiny green peas

1¾ ounces escarole, chopped

1¾ ounces bitter greens, chopped

2 celery stalks, chopped

2 carrots, chopped

1 pig's foot

1 pig's ear

3½ ounces prosciutto

5½ ounces pork rind

1 sprig of marjoram

1 sprig of mint

3 tablespoons extra-virgin olive oil

2 ounces pork fat, chopped

2 garlic cloves

1 medium onion, chopped

1 tablespoon chopped fresh
Italian parsley

1 teaspoon dried hot
pepper

4 ripe medium plum tomatoes,
peeled, seeded, and chopped

Fine sea salt and freshly
ground black pepper

5¼ ounces assorted dry pasta

¼ cup freshly grated pecorino cheese

1. Cook the soaked beans for 1 hour, or until they are tender, in a large pot filled
with enough salted cold water to cover them.

2. In the meantime, in a large skillet cook the fava beans, peas, escarole, and bitter greens in a small amount of salted water for 1 hour. Add the celery and carrots and cook for about 10 minutes, until they are tender.

3. In a very large pot, boil the pig's foot, pig's ear, prosciutto, and pork rind in
water to cover for about 1 hour. Drain, debone, and chop the meat. Strain the
cooking liquid and return to the pot with the meat pieces. Add the boiled beans,
the marjoram, and mint and cook for 30 minutes.

4. In a large skillet, brown the olive oil and the chopped pork fat with the garlic,
onion, chopped parsley, and dried hot pepper. Add the tomatoes and cook for 10
minutes. Pour this sauce and the fava bean mixture into the pot of meat and

cook for a few minutes. Adjust the seasoning with salt and pepper.

5. In abundant salted water, cook the dry pasta until al dente. Add to the soup.

6. Ladle the soup into individual dishes and sprinkle with pecorino cheese.

SERVES 6

Minestra di lenticchie

LENTIL SOUP

The Bible tells of Esau selling his inheritance to Jacob for a dish of lentils;
this soup illustrates why they were considered so valuable.

3 cups dry Italian lentils, soaked for 3 hours and drained	2 celery stalks, finely chopped
Extra-virgin olive oil	1 garlic clove, finely chopped
2 sprigs of rosemary	3½-ounce slab of Italian prosciutto (with the fat)
2 garlic cloves	1 tablespoon tomato paste
1 bay leaf	⅓ cup dry white wine
1 carrot, finely chopped	Fine sea salt and freshly ground black pepper
½ medium onion, finely chopped	

1. In a large pot, with cold salted water to cover, combine the lentils, 2 tablespoons olive oil, 1 rosemary sprig, 2 whole garlic cloves, and the bay leaf, and cook for about 1 hour over medium heat, until the lentils are tender.

2. In a large heavy saucepan, heat 4 tablespoons of olive oil. Add the carrot, onion, celery, garlic, 1 rosemary sprig, and prosciutto; cook for 15 minutes over medium heat. Add the tomato paste and wine; cook until the wine evaporates.

3. Drain a little more than half of the lentils and add to the pan. Place the remaining lentils with the cooking liquid in a food processor. Process until smooth. Add to the pan and cook for 30 minutes over low heat, stirring frequently.

4. Before serving, remove the prosciutto. Ladle the soup into individual dishes and serve with a drizzle of olive oil, salt, and freshly ground pepper.

SERVES 6

Salads

ANY RESTAURANT that prides itself on serving light fare must offer a compelling array of salads, and Mezzaluna is no exception to this rule. Our salads are among the most popular offerings on the menu. Because our customers often order a salad as the focus of their meal, perhaps accompanied by a bowl of soup for lunch or followed by a shared pasta or pizza for dinner, I wanted to create salads that were more substantial and offered more flavor and textural excitement than a simple mixed green or tricolor salad. The Mezzaluna salad, for example, contrasts the silky, elusive flavor of thinly sliced raw artichoke with piquant Parmesan cheese. ❂ Except for a few traditional regional salads, such as the Tuscan *panzanella*, a peasant ode to resourcefulness made with leftover bread, and the Taormina featuring the famed Sicilian oranges, most of the salads at Mezzaluna are a product of the chefs' and my whimsy. I love to combine typical Italian ingredients such as capers, olives, tuna, regional cheeses, and cured meats with a variety of greens and vegetables to make surprising new flavors. The salad menu also borrows from different cultures, and hearts of palm and avocados are used freely. All of our salads are seasoned with extra-virgin olive oil, a splash of balsamic vinegar, and freshly ground black pepper. Any of these salads will bring a bit of our beloved Mediterranean sun to your table.

Insalata Mezzaluna

MEZZALUNA SALAD

*I created this salad when I opened the original Mezzaluna
restaurant in New York over ten years ago. It was an immediate success
and remains on the menu to this day. It can be eaten year-round
and is unusual for its use of thinly sliced raw artichokes.*

1 lemon

1 pound baby artichokes

1 pound white mushrooms

3 celery stalks with leaves

¾ pound mixed greens,
washed and dried

1 bunch arugula, cleaned and dried,
tough stems removed

1 cup shaved Parmesan cheese

5 tablespoons extra-virgin olive oil

2 tablespoons balsamic vinegar

Fine sea salt and freshly ground
black pepper

2 tablespoons finely chopped chives

1. Squeeze the lemon into a medium bowl filled with water.

2. Remove the tough outer leaves from the artichokes and trim off the leaf tips.
Cut the artichokes in half and cut out the choke with a small knife. Drop into
the acidulated water to prevent darkening.

3. Clean the mushrooms with a soft brush and trim the stems. Rinse the mushrooms quickly under cold running water. Gently pat dry with a soft towel. Slice
the mushrooms a quarter inch thick.

4. Remove the leaves from the celery stalks and reserve. Slice the stalks thinly.
Drain the artichokes and slice very thinly with a very sharp knife.

5. On 4 serving plates, arrange a bed of greens and arugula. Top with the celery,
mushrooms, the shaved Parmesan, and the sliced artichokes.

6. In a small bowl, whisk together the olive oil, balsamic vinegar, and salt and
pepper. Drizzle the salad with the dressing and then sprinkle each salad with the
chopped chives and reserved celery leaves.

SERVES 4

Insalata Taormina

This salad originates in Sicily, where large groves of oranges have been cultivated since the end of the eighteenth century. Because oranges were so abundant, peasants combined slices with local vegetables and ate them with olive oil, salt, and pepper. Mezzaluna's version, created by Francesca Cianchi, introduces the distinctive taste of endive and an olive sauce for a smoother and more palatable dish.

2 medium fennel bulbs	¼ cup extra-virgin olive oil
4 heads Belgian endive	Juice of ½ lemon
3 oranges	Fine sea salt and freshly
½ cup coarsely chopped walnuts	ground black pepper
2 tablespoons olive paste (olivada)	

1. Chop the fennel. Cut the endives lengthwise into long strips.

2. Using a sharp knife, cut the rinds off the oranges, removing all the white pith. Slice the oranges crosswise in thin slices.

3. On individual plates, arrange the oranges, fennel, and endive. Sprinkle with the walnuts.

4. In a small bowl, combine the olive paste with the olive oil and lemon juice. Drizzle over the salad and season with salt and pepper to taste.

SERVES 4

Insalata Pantesca

POTATO, TUNA FISH, CAPER, ONION, AND TOMATO SALAD

*Pantelleria is a small island southwest of Sicily famous for its capers, both
wild and cultivated. They have a wonderful Mediterranean aroma and flavor,
which is best preserved when they are cured in salt. Our Pantesca salad is a
variation of the Provençal* pan bagnat, *with capers the prevailing flavor.*

5 tablespoons Pantelleria capers,
preserved in salt

3 Yukon gold potatoes,
peeled and cubed

5 tablespoons plus 1 teaspoon
extra-virgin olive oil

2 fresh sage leaves

1 tablespoon balsamic vinegar

Fine sea salt and freshly
ground black pepper

2 bunches mâche (lamb's lettuce),
trimmed, washed, and dried

4 plum tomatoes, quartered

1 cucumber, sliced

1 onion, thinly sliced into rings

2 6-ounce cans of tuna in
olive oil, drained

32 black Ligurian or Niçoise olives

1 tablespoon chopped fresh basil

1. Soak the capers in 2 cups of lukewarm water for 20 minutes, changing the
water 2 or 3 times. Drain.

2. Clean, peel, and cube the potatoes. Place in a saucepan with 2 cups salted
water, 1 teaspoon of olive oil, and the sage leaves. Bring to a boil, then reduce the
heat and simmer for about 5 minutes. Drain and set aside.

3. In a small bowl, whisk together the remaining 5 tablespoons of olive oil, the
balsamic vinegar, and salt and pepper. In a salad bowl, combine the capers,
mâche, tomatoes, cucumber, onion, tuna, and olives and toss with the dressing.
Alternatively, arrange the ingredients on individual plates, alternating tomato,
mâche, cucumber, onion, and tuna. Top with the capers, olives, and chopped basil
and drizzle with the dressing.

SERVES 4

Insalata Pontormo

SALAD OF APPLE, SPECK, *FRISÉE*, AND ASIAGO CHEESE

Pontormo, whose likeness is the logo of our sister restaurant, Mezzogiorno, was a Renaissance painter who kept a journal of his gastronomic experiments. This recipe is a modern variation on one of his old recipes that combines apple and cheese with cured meat. Speck is a kind of smoked prosciutto available in the northern regions of Italy, especially in Alto Adige and Friuli on the Austrian border. If you cannot locate a source for speck, substitute regular prosciutto.

LEMON DRESSING
⅓ cup (6 tablespoons) extra-virgin olive oil

Juice of 1 lemon

1 teaspoon grated lemon rind

1 red Cortland or McIntosh apple, sliced

¼ pound speck or prosciutto, cut in strips

¼ pound Asiago cheese, diced

2 bunches *frisée* lettuce

1 bunch mâche (lamb's lettuce)

Fine sea salt and freshly ground black pepper

1. In a small bowl, whisk together the olive oil, lemon juice, and lemon rind.

2. Core the unpeeled apple and slice very thin. Cut the speck into thin strips. Cut the Asiago into small dice.

3. In a serving bowl, combine the *frisée* and mâche with the apple, speck, and cheese. Toss well with the lemon dressing and season with salt and pepper to taste.

SERVES 4

MEZZOGIORNO

Insalata Miró

PEAR, GORGONZOLA CHEESE, MIXED GREENS, AND WALNUT SALAD

Vittorio Ansuini, my partner at Mezzogiorno, created this salad in the fall of 1994, when New York's Museum of Modern Art had an exhibition of the art of the Spanish painter Miró. It was an homage to a devoted group of customers from Barcelona.

Juice of 1 lemon	VINAIGRETTE
4 medium Bartlett or Anjou pears, ripe but firm	4 tablespoons extra-virgin olive oil
	1 teaspoon white wine vinegar
3 ounces aged Gorgonzola cheese	Splash of champagne
	Fine sea salt and freshly
1 pound mixed greens	ground black pepper
½ cup walnut halves	

1. Squeeze the lemon into a medium bowl filled with water. Peel the pears and place in the acidulated water for 2 minutes. Cut the Gorgonzola into thin logs as long as the pears. Core the pears and fill the cavities with the Gorgonzola logs. Cut the pears crosswise into 1-inch slices.

2. Combine the vinaigrette ingredients in a bowl.

3. On 4 individual plates, arrange the stuffed pear slices in a fan. Place a portion of the greens on each plate and sprinkle with walnuts. Drizzle the salads with the vinaigrette.

SERVES 4

NOTE: You may also serve the stuffed pear whole, placing it in the center of the individual plate, with a portion of the greens and topped with walnuts and vinaigrette.

Insalata Isabella

RENAISSANCE CHICKEN SALAD

In 1489, this recipe was served to five hundred guests at the wedding banquet of Isabel of Aragon and Gian Galeazzo Sforza, an Italian nobleman. It is still a most elegant dish. At that time, capon was used instead of chicken.

1 3-pound chicken	Juice of 2 lemons
1 carrot, peeled	½ cup raisins
1 onion	2 small apples
2 celery stalks	¾ pound celery hearts
1 bunch parsley	1 small fennel bulb
2 garlic cloves, peeled	5 tablespoons Sicilian capers, preserved in salt
4 to 5 whole black peppercorns	
1 teaspoon salt	Fine sea salt and freshly ground black pepper
10 tablespoons extra-virgin olive oil	2 bunches *frisée* lettuce

1. Place the chicken in a saucepan or skillet with the carrot, onion, celery stalks, parsley, garlic cloves, peppercorns, salt, and water to just cover. Bring to a boil, then reduce the heat and simmer gently for about 1 hour, until the chicken is cooked; remove the chicken to a plate and cool. Discard the skin and bones and cut the chicken in strips. Combine 6 tablespoons of the olive oil and the juice of 1½ lemons in a mixing bowl. Add the chicken, toss, and chill for 2 hours.

2. Soak the raisins in lukewarm water for 30 minutes to soften. Meanwhile, peel and core the apples and cut into thin slices. Slice the celery and fennel thinly. In another bowl, soak the capers in lukewarm water for 20 minutes to remove the salt.

3. Just before serving, drain the raisins and capers and toss together with the chicken. Add the apples, celery, and fennel. Whisk together the remaining 4 tablespoons olive oil, the juice of ½ lemon, and salt and pepper, and toss with the salad.

4. Make beds of the *frisée* on individual plates. Top with a portion of the chicken salad and serve cold.

SERVES 6 TO 8

Panzanella

The very resourceful wives of the Tuscan peasants improvised this dish with leftover bread combined with odds and ends of vegetables. At noon, when the sun shone hot on the fields and the men took a break by the irrigating ditches called zanellas, *their women would bring the bread, hence the name* panzanella, *or "bread by the ditches."*

1 pound stale Tuscan or other dense white bread (at least several days old)	4 radishes, sliced
1 cup extra-virgin olive oil	6 ripe medium tomatoes, quartered
5 tablespoons red wine vinegar	20 fresh basil leaves
2 red onions, sliced	Fine sea salt and freshly ground black pepper
1½ cucumbers, peeled and sliced	

1. In a large bowl, soak the bread slices in 3 cups of cold water for about 15 minutes. With your hands, carefully squeeze the water out of the bread pieces, making sure they are thoroughly dry, and crumble them into a large bowl.

2. Add ¾ cup of olive oil and 1 tablespoon red wine vinegar.

3. Add the onions, cucumber slices, radishes, and tomatoes. With your hands, tear the basil leaves in two and add to the salad. Season with salt and pepper and mix, preferably with your hands. Refrigerate until ready to serve.

4. Just before serving, add the rest of the vinegar and drizzle with the remaining olive oil.

SERVES 4

VARIATION: You can make a dark panzanella with dark bread; add sliced fennel, carrots, and celery stalks and leaves.

Costa Smeralda

CRABMEAT, AVOCADO, TOMATO, RADICCHIO, AND MÂCHE SALAD

The fashionable Costa Smeralda resort in northern Sardinia inspired this refreshing salad, introduced to me by my old friend and partner Romano Molfetta. It is very popular in our restaurant in Corona del Mar, California. Serve with dark toasted bread and a glass of Prosecco.

1 bunch mâche (lamb's lettuce)	2 tomatoes, cut in wedges
1 head radicchio	6 tablespoons extra-virgin olive oil
1 pound lump crabmeat, picked over (see Note)	Juice of 1 lemon
2 avocados, sliced	Fine sea salt and freshly ground black pepper

1. Trim the roots off the mâche and wash and dry thoroughly. Divide among 4 serving plates. Core the radicchio and cut into thin shreds.

2. Mound one-fourth of the crabmeat and shredded radicchio on each bed of mâche and surround with some of the avocado slices and tomato wedges.

3. In a small bowl, whisk together the olive oil, lemon juice, and salt and pepper. Drizzle over the salads and serve.

SERVES 4

NOTE: When in season, freshly cooked crabmeat makes this salad even more special. Boil 10 to 12 live blue crabs in abundant salted water for 20 minutes, then cool and remove the meat from the shell with a nutcracker or mallet.

Insalata Toscana

BEEF, POTATO, RED ONION, AND PARSLEY SALAD

The peasants of Tuscany have created many memorable dishes from leftovers, among them this delicious and hearty salad that has become a menu staple at many an Italian trattoria. This mixture of cubed beef and boiled potatoes, enlivened with some fresh parsley and extra-virgin olive oil, is a good example of the authentic regional cuisine that Mezzaluna serves and promotes.

1 pound brisket of beef	3 fresh sage leaves
4 cups beef broth	1 tablespoon red wine vinegar
2 cups red wine	Fine sea salt and freshly ground black pepper
½ onion, chopped	
1 carrot, sliced	1 teaspoon crumbled dried hot pepper
1 celery stalk	
1 bay leaf	2 teaspoons Dijon mustard
6 medium Yukon gold potatoes	1 red onion, coarsely chopped
⅓ cup plus 2 teaspoons extra-virgin olive oil	2 peeled plum tomatoes, finely diced
	½ cup chopped fresh Italian parsley

1. Place the meat in a large saucepan with the beef broth, wine, onion, carrot, celery, and bay leaf. Bring to a boil over high heat, then reduce the heat to medium, cover, and simmer for 2 hours. Drain the meat. When cool enough to handle, cut the meat into ½-inch cubes and set aside.

2. Meanwhile, scrub, peel, and dice the potatoes. Place in a saucepan with 4 cups of salted water, 2 teaspoons of the olive oil, and the sage leaves. Bring to a boil, then simmer for 5 minutes. Drain and set aside.

3. In a small bowl, whisk together the remaining olive oil, vinegar, salt and pepper, dried hot pepper, and Dijon mustard.

4. In a large bowl, combine the cubed meat, diced potatoes, red onion, tomatoes, and chopped parsley. Add the dressing and toss well.

SERVES 4

Insalata Chiantigiana

FRISÉE, CACIOTTA CHEESE, PANCETTA, AND POACHED EGG SALAD

*During harvest time in the Chianti region, peasants spent long hours in
the vineyards. To lighten their day, the women prepared this appealing and
simple cold salad, which features caciotta, a mild sheep's milk cheese. A
similar tradition exists in France, in the Beaujolais region. I have added
the poached egg to enhance the flavors and give it a sunny touch.*

5 ounces pancetta, cut in strips	2 bunches *frisée* lettuce
¼ cup extra-virgin olive oil	4 eggs
1 tablespoon balsamic vinegar	5 ounces caciotta cheese
Fine sea salt and freshly ground pepper	1 cup croutons

1. In a heavy skillet, cook the pancetta slowly, over medium heat, until it is crispy. Drain the pancetta on paper towels or place it on bread slices to absorb excess fat.

2. In a large bowl, whisk together the vinegar, olive oil, and salt and pepper to taste. Add the *frisée* and toss well.

3. Bring a shallow pan of water to a simmer. Carefully slide in the eggs and poach gently for 3 minutes or to taste.

4. While the eggs poach, arrange the dressed *frisée* on 4 serving plates. Place a poached egg in the center of each and surround it with some of the cheese, pancetta, and croutons.

SERVES 4

Insalata Tropicale

TROPICAL SALAD

As a departure from Italian culture or tradition, I created this tropical salad that incorporates avocado and hearts of palm, ingredients that have become available in every market. Always in demand, it has been on our menu for more than ten years.

1 bunch *frisée* lettuce	Fine sea salt and freshly ground black pepper
2 ripe avocados, sliced	1 cup shaved Parmesan cheese
10 hearts of palm, sliced	5 chives
2 plum tomatoes, diced	Arugula leaves
5 tablespoons extra-virgin olive oil	
Juice of ½ lemon	

1. Clean and trim the *frisée,* discarding any wilted leaves. Rinse the salad well and dry in a salad spinner.

2. Halve both avocados and remove the pits. Peel and cut in thin slices. Drain the hearts of palm and slice thinly.

3. Core the tomatoes and dice very finely.

4. In a bowl, whisk together the olive oil, lemon juice, and salt and pepper.

5. Arrange the *frisée* on individual plates. Arrange the diced tomato, avocado slices, and hearts of palm on top in a decorative manner. Drizzle with the salad dressing and top with the Parmesan cheese shavings. Sprinkle with chopped chives and place some arugula leaves on top.

SERVES 4

Insalata Mezzogiorno

SHRIMP AND CAPER SALAD

In Italian, mezzogiorno *has two meanings: noon and the southern regions*
of Italy, which are the sunniest. This salad was created for Mezzogiorno,
Mezzaluna's sister restaurant located in downtown Manhattan. The capers
give it a Mediterranean and southern Italian flavor. Use the smallest capers,
as they are far tastier than the large ones. By the way, capers should never
be cooked, as they lose their aroma and become bitter.

4 tablespoons Sicilian capers,
preserved in salt

10 baby artichokes or 10 frozen
artichoke hearts, thawed

1½ pounds medium shrimp
(about 32)

2 bay leaves

Whole white peppercorns

6 tablespoons extra-virgin olive oil

1 garlic clove, pressed

½ cup chopped fresh Italian parsley

1 lemon, sliced

6 Oven-Roasted Tomatoes,
coarsely chopped (page 110)

1 teaspoon white wine vinegar

Fine sea salt and freshly
ground black pepper

1. Soak the capers in 2 cups of lukewarm water for 20 minutes, changing the
water 2 or 3 times.

2. Remove the tough outer leaves of the artichokes and trim off the leaf tips.
Cut the artichokes in half and cut out the choke with a small knife. Bring abundant salted water to a boil. Drop in the artichokes and cook for about 10 minutes,
until they are tender. Drain and allow to cool. Cut into fine strips.

3. Cook the shrimp in abundant boiling water for a few minutes, adding the
bay leaves and a few white peppercorns. Drain, shell, and place in a large bowl.
While the shrimp are still warm, season with 5 tablespoons of olive oil, garlic,
parsley, and capers.

4. Place the shrimp in the center of a platter and surround them with the artichokes, lemon slices, and roasted tomatoes. Sprinkle with the vinegar and the
remaining tablespoon of olive oil. Season with salt and pepper and serve.

SERVES 4

Carpaccios

✿

CARPACCIO was created by the famous restaurateur Giuseppe Cipriani, owner of the celebrated Harry's Bar in Venice, in response to a request by a frequent guest whose doctor had recommended a special diet that included raw meat. Mr. Cipriani came up with the idea of slicing a raw fillet of beef paper thin, like prosciutto, and sprinkling it with a flavored mayonnaise. At the time, an exhibition in Venice was showing the works of the great Renaissance painter Carpaccio. The colors of the dish recalled certain characteristics of the painter's work, and Mr. Cipriani named his invention after him. ✦ Today, carpaccio refers to any thinly sliced raw meats, including veal as well as beef, and even fish, such as salmon. At Mezzaluna we serve several carpaccios year-round, and even offer what we call hot carpaccios, which are actually fast-seared rather than completely raw. ✦ The key to making a fine carpaccio is slicing the meat paper thin in nearly transparent sheets, a process that is made much simpler by partially freezing the meat for about 1 hour before slicing. Use a very well honed knife to shave off the slices, then arrange them neatly on serving dishes and allow the meat to return to room temperature for 15 minutes before serving. You may need to blot off any meat juices that accumulate as the meat thaws; simply pat with a paper towel, then garnish as directed in the recipe. Do, by all means, try this elegantly simple preparation at home.

Carpaccio rucola e parmigiano

CARPACCIO WITH ARUGULA AND PARMESAN

A carpaccio that became very popular in Milan, this is a variation
of the classic version served at Harry's Bar in Venice.

12-ounce beef tenderloin in one piece	**4 to 6 tablespoons extra-virgin olive oil**
½ pound arugula, rinsed and tough stems trimmed	**Fine sea salt and freshly ground black pepper**
6 ounces Parmesan cheese shavings	**2 lemons, halved**

1. Wrap the beef tenderloin in plastic wrap and place in the freezer for 2 hours. Remove the plastic wrap and, using a very sharp butcher knife, cut the meat into paper-thin slices. Cover 4 individual plates with the carpaccio slices.

2. Top each plate with one-quarter of the arugula and Parmesan shavings. Drizzle with olive oil, season with salt and pepper, and serve with a lemon half on the side.

SERVES 4

Carpaccio al sapore di mare

TASTE OF THE SEA CARPACCIO

A great appetizer in the summertime, this is an unusual carpaccio, with anchovies in the sauce providing an interesting contrast to the meat. The anchovies are practically dissolved and their subtle presence adds a particular aroma to the dish. Try it with a good bottle of Pinot Bianco from Friuli.

12-ounce beef tenderloin in one piece	4 tablespoons extra-virgin olive oil
5 Italian anchovy fillets preserved in olive oil, finely chopped	1 teaspoon chopped fresh chili pepper
Juice of 2 lemons	Fine sea salt and freshly ground black pepper
1 garlic clove, minced	
3 tablespoons finely chopped fresh Italian parsley	Parsley, for garnish
	Lemon wedges, for garnish

1. Wrap the beef tenderloin in plastic wrap and place in the freezer for 2 hours. With a very sharp butcher knife, cut it into paper-thin slices. Cover 4 serving plates with the carpaccio slices.

2. Place the chopped anchovy fillets in a small bowl. Add the lemon juice, garlic, parsley, olive oil, and chili pepper. Season with the salt and pepper and whisk vigorously until well blended.

3. Brush the sauce over the carpaccio slices and allow to rest in the refrigerator for at least 2 hours. Sprinkle with more salt and pepper. Garnish with the parsley and lemon wedges.

SERVES 4

Carpaccio Margherita

CARPACCIO WITH MOZZARELLA, TOMATO, AND BASIL

Pizza Margherita inspired this colorful carpaccio, which gives the classic
ingredients of tomato, mozzarella, and basil an innovative new twist.

12-ounce beef tenderloin in one piece

2 plum tomatoes, diced

2 tablespoons chopped fresh basil

1 tablespoon chopped fresh oregano

4 to 6 tablespoons extra-
virgin olive oil

1 tablespoon balsamic vinegar

Fine sea salt and freshly
ground black pepper

6 ounces fresh mozzarella cheese,
cut in ¼-inch dice

1. Wrap the beef tenderloin in plastic wrap and place in the freezer for 2 hours.
Cut into paper-thin slices with a well-sharpened butcher knife. Cover 4 individual plates with the carpaccio slices.

2. In a small bowl, combine the tomatoes, basil, and oregano. Stir in 4 tablespoons of the olive oil, the balsamic vinegar, and salt and pepper to taste. Let
stand for 10 minutes.

3. Spoon the tomato mixture over the carpaccio slices. Top with the diced
mozzarella, drizzle on the remaining olive oil, and adjust the seasoning with
salt and pepper.

SERVES 4

Carpaccio con avocado e palmito

I have introduced two exotic elements, avocado and hearts of palm,
to this carpaccio to make a pleasant and different combination.

12-ounce beef tenderloin in one piece	Fine sea salt and freshly ground black pepper
2 avocados	6 tablespoons extra-virgin olive oil
4 hearts of palm	2 lemons, halved
1 cup mixed greens	

1. Wrap the beef tenderloin in plastic wrap and place in the freezer for 2 hours. With a very sharp butcher knife, cut it into paper-thin slices. Cover 4 individual plates with the carpaccio slices. Let stand at room temperature for 15 minutes; blot any meat juices that accumulate with a paper towel.

2. Peel and slice the avocados on the diagonal. Slice the hearts of palm on the diagonal into 6 pieces. Top the carpaccio with alternating slices of avocado and hearts of palm. Place a mound of greens in the middle of each plate. Season with salt and pepper, drizzle with olive oil, and serve with a lemon half on the side.

SERVES 4

Carpaccio con gorgonzola e noci

CARPACCIO WITH GORGONZOLA CHEESE AND WALNUTS

This dish is an improvisation on the classic French salad featuring Roquefort cheese and walnuts. In adapting it to a carpaccio, I have substituted Gorgonzola, which I find to be creamier and more flavorful than its French counterpart.

12-ounce beef tenderloin in one piece	1 tablespoon chopped fresh Italian parsley
1 cup *frisée* lettuce, well washed	4 to 6 tablespoons extra-virgin olive oil
3½ ounces aged Gorgonzola cheese, crumbled	Fine sea salt and freshly ground black pepper
⅓ cup coarsely chopped walnuts	2 lemons, halved

1. Wrap the beef tenderloin in plastic wrap and place in the freezer for 2 hours. With a very sharp butcher knife, cut it into paper-thin slices.

2. Cover 4 individual plates with the carpaccio slices. Place a mound of *frisée* in the center of each plate. Crumble the cheese over the carpaccio and top with a sprinkle of walnuts and parsley and a drizzle of olive oil. Season with salt and pepper. Serve with a lemon half on the side.

SERVES 4

Carpaccio caldo Pizzaiola

HOT CARPACCIO WITH TOMATOES, OLIVES, AND OREGANO

Carpacci "caldi" grew out of my desire to offer at Mezzaluna a meat-based second course that is very light and at the same time appetizing and amusing. To make the dish more appealing to those who are hesitant to eat raw meat, the meat is "scottata" (burned) in a skillet for just a few seconds. The toppings vary according to the seasons and the availability of ingredients.

14-ounce beef tenderloin in one piece	1 tablespoon chopped fresh oregano
½ cup extra-virgin olive oil	½ cup pitted black Ligurian olives
2 garlic cloves, chopped	Fine sea salt and freshly ground black pepper
4 cups peeled, seeded, and finely chopped fresh plum tomatoes (about 1 pound)	1 tablespoon chopped fresh basil

1. Wrap the beef tenderloin in plastic wrap and place in the freezer for 2 hours. Cut into ⅛-inch slices with a well-sharpened butcher knife.

2. In a heavy skillet, heat 2 tablespoons of olive oil until it is very hot. Add the beef slices and sear for 5 seconds on each side over a very high flame. Work in batches and do not crowd the pan or the beef will not sear properly. Transfer the slices to a platter and set aside.

3. Heat the remaining olive oil in the skillet, add the garlic, tomatoes, oregano, and black olives, and sauté for about a minute. Season with salt and pepper.

4. Cover 4 individual plates with the carpaccio slices and top with the sauce. Sprinkle with the basil and serve warm.

SERVES 4

Carpaccio caldo Ortolano

HOT CARPACCIO WITH GRILLED VEGETABLES

Simple and healthy, this meat-and-vegetable carpaccio is particularly convenient as a last-minute meal. Use a variety of colorful vegetables.

14-ounce beef tenderloin in one piece

½ medium eggplant or 2 Japanese eggplants

Fine sea salt

1 carrot

2 small zucchini

½ fennel bulb, sliced

6 small shiitake mushrooms, stems removed

1 Belgian endive

4 to 6 tablespoons extra-virgin olive oil

Freshly ground black pepper

12 fresh basil leaves, chopped

1. Wrap the beef tenderloin in plastic wrap and place in the freezer for 2 hours. Cut into ⅛-inch slices with a sharp butcher knife.

2. Trim the ends of the eggplant. Cut crosswise into very thin slices, season with salt, and set aside in a colander until it releases its water, about 20 to 30 minutes.

3. In the meantime, trim and peel the carrot. Slice at an angle about ⅛ inch thick. Trim the zucchini and slice at an angle about ⅛ inch thick. Remove the outer layer of the fennel and cut the core into ¼-inch slices. Wipe the mushroom caps with a damp towel. Rinse the endive and split lengthwise. Rinse the eggplant slices briefly and pat them dry.

4. Heat a ridged iron grill pan and brush it with olive oil. Grill all the vegetables for 3 minutes on each side, transferring to a platter as they are done. Set aside and keep warm.

5. In a heavy skillet, heat 2 tablespoons of olive oil. Sauté the beef slices over high heat for 10 seconds on each side, working in batches if necessary. Transfer to the platter. Season with salt and freshly ground pepper.

6. Cover 4 individual plates with the carpaccio slices. Arrange the grilled vegetables decoratively on top of the carpaccio. Drizzle with olive oil, season with salt and pepper, and garnish with the chopped basil.

SERVES 4

Carpaccio caldo Valligiano

HOT CARPACCIO WITH FONTINA AND PROSCIUTTO

*While carpaccio is associated primarily with warm weather in this country,
in Italy it is eaten year-round. This is a hearty and flavorful carpaccio for the cold
season. Melted fontina gives this version its special character. Truffle-flavored
oil, a less costly alternative to the real thing, adds an earthy aroma.*

14-ounce beef tenderloin in one piece, trimmed	**12 thin slices fontina cheese**
1 tablespoon extra-virgin olive oil	**12 thin slices speck (smoked prosciutto) or regular prosciutto**
Fine sea salt and freshly ground black pepper	**4 tablespoons truffled olive oil**

1. Wrap the beef tenderloin in plastic wrap and place in the freezer for 2 hours.
With a well-sharpened knife, cut it into ⅛-inch slices.

2. In a heavy skillet, heat the olive oil. Sear the meat slices over high heat
for 10 seconds on each side. Cook the meat in batches without overcrowding
the pan and transfer the slices to a platter as they are cooked. Season with salt
and pepper.

3. On 4 individual plates, alternate the carpaccio slices with 3 slices of fontina
cheese and 3 slices of speck per person. Drizzle with the truffled oil. Season with
more freshly ground pepper.

SERVES 4

Pasta

✳

*I*F THE NAME MEZZALUNA has become synonymous with pasta it's because this versatile food, whether baked or boiled, fresh or dried, stuffed or not, is the heart of our cuisine. Today, there are many restaurants— not all of them Italian!—offering main-course pastas, but when our restaurant first opened its doors this was a rather unconventional concept. Traditionally, pastas were served as a first course, preceding a more substantial meat or fish course. We made pasta the star of the show and it has been basking in the spotlight of popularity ever since. ❁ Few foods reflect our commitment to using fresh, authentic, and seasonal ingredients better than our pastas. At the restaurant we offer more than a dozen pastas in addition to daily lasagne and ravioli specials. Many of these have been signature dishes from the start of Mezzaluna; *rigatoni con melanzane e ricotta salata* and our black linguine with spicy *sciue sciue* sauce have developed such devoted followings that I have learned to keep them on the menu year-round. The majority, however, are seasonal offerings that may reappear year after year but are only available when their ingredients are at their peak. ❁ During the warm months, Mezzaluna's pasta dishes are light, colorful, and refreshing. Our spaghetti with raw summer vegetables is a typical improvisation that can be eaten hot or cold. In the wintertime we suggest heartier fare, such as shells with a rich lentil and sausage *ragù* or pappardelle with earthy porcinis and truffles. The recipes that follow have been divided into four groups, one for each of the seasons, just as we prepare them at the restaurant. ❋ The great French gastronome Auguste Escoffier remarked that cooking pasta is an art, and as such must be learned and cultivated. To Italians, it is a sacred ritual complete with tips passed down from generation to generation. While there are certain regional variations, the five "golden rules of pasta" that follow are the basic tenets of a well-cooked pasta. They reflect the way we prepare every plate of pasta that we serve at Mezzaluna. ❋ 1. USE THE PROPER EQUIPMENT. Your pot should be large enough to contain *an abundant amount* of water so the pasta can swim freely in the water, $4\frac{1}{2}$ quarts for every pound of pasta cooked. Stainless steel pans conduct heat most evenly; those that come with a strainer insert are especially convenient. ❋ 2. USE TOP-QUALITY INGREDIENTS. Our recipes use both fresh and dry pastas. For dry, select imported Italian pastas made from 100 percent durum semolina. I prefer those made by small producers, such as Latini and Martelli, which use old bronze molds and traditional methods to make the pasta. ❋ Fresh pastas, such as those used for tagliolini and pappardelle, are now widely available and are generally of acceptable quality. However, pasta is quite easily made at home and for certain dishes—fresh ravioli or squid ink pasta, to name two—it is indispensable. Purchased sheets of fresh pasta can certainly be used for lasagne when time is tight, but these will not be thin enough for ravioli. ❋ 3. BOIL THE PASTA CORRECTLY. Cook pasta in cold tap water that has been brought to a rapid boil over medium heat. The relatively

low heat will enable you to raise the flame and thus maintain the boil after the pasta has been added. Once the water reaches the boiling point *add a generous amount of fine sea salt*—about 2 teaspoons per quart of water. Do not add oil to the water; contrary to popular opinion, this does not prevent the pasta from sticking and is just a waste of good oil.

Add the pasta to the water gradually if it is a short, dry shape. If it is a long, dry pasta, twist the strands into the pot, pushing any exposed ends under the water with a wooden spoon; never break the pasta. Raise the heat to return the water to a boil and stir the pasta while it cooks to keep it from sticking.

4. DON'T OVERCOOK. Pasta should always be cooked al dente. Italians believe that the firmer bite of al dente pasta requires the diner to chew more thoroughly, rendering it more digestible. Whether or not this is true, a plate of firm, separate strands or individual shaped pastas is certainly more appetizing than the gluey, sticky, formless mush that pasta can become with only a minute or two of overcooking. It is impossible to set any hard and fast rules for cooking time as it varies according to the shape and whether the pasta is fresh or dried. However, as a general guideline, long dry pasta cooks in 6 to 10 minutes and short pasta shapes require 10 to 15 minutes.

As soon as the pasta is cooked, add a cup of cold water to the pot to stop the cooking process (the pasta will continue to cook as it sits in the hot water, even off the flame) and drain immediately. If you are cooking fresh pasta sheets such as lasagna or pappardelle, stir in a bit of olive oil before draining; this is an exception to rule 3 and does, in fact, prevent the sheets from sticking together.

5. The final and most important rule is the golden secret to all of our pasta dishes: COOK THE PASTA AND SAUCE TOGETHER BRIEFLY JUST BEFORE SERVING. Heat (or reheat) the sauce in the skillet it was prepared in. Add the drained pasta, raise the heat to very high, and sauté for 30 seconds, tossing or stirring constantly. The process melds the sauce to the pasta, brings out all the flavors, and ensures the dish will arrive on the table piping hot.

Follow these rules, and follow the seasons, and a perfect plate of pasta is all but guaranteed.

Spring

MINIGONNE ALL'ISOLANA
Minigonne with tomatoes, capers, olives, and spicy sauce

TRITTICO DI PASTA CORTA CON SUGO DI TONNO PICCANTE
Trio of short pasta in spicy tuna sauce

MACCHERONCINI CON CARCIOFI E ROSMARINO
Maccheroncini with artichokes and rosemary

FUSILLI CON LATTUGA E PUNTE DI ASPARAGI
Fusilli with lettuce and asparagus tips

TROFIETTE AL MEZZO PESTO E FAGIOLINI
Trofiette with half pesto and string beans

TRENETTE PREZZEMOLATE CON VONGOLE E OLIVE NERE
Parsley trenette with clams and black olives

RAVIOLI CON ZUCCHINE E POMODORI SECCHI
Ravioli with zucchini and sun-dried tomatoes

RAVIOLI NERI AI GRANCHI
Black ravioli with crabmeat

STROZZAPRETI CON CIPOLLOTTO E PEPERONCINO
Strozzapreti with spring onion and chili paste

RAVIOLI CON SPINACI E RICOTTA
Ravioli with spinach and ricotta

Minigonne all'isolana

MINIGONNE WITH TOMATOES, CAPERS, OLIVES, AND SPICY SAUCE

*Isolana means "island style." Found in the islands of southern
Italy where capers and sun-dried tomatoes are widely available, this
dish captures all the flavors of the Mediterranean. Minigonne, meaning
"miniskirts," is the name I've given to this short-cut maccheroncino.
Fusilli would work equally well.*

¼ cup extra-virgin olive oil

1 garlic clove, chopped

½ cup chopped shallots
(about 3 to 4)

2 Italian anchovy fillets,
packed in olive oil

½ cup Sicilian capers,
preserved in salt

⅓ cup pitted black Ligurian olives

½ cup Ligurian sun-dried tomatoes,
or other oil-packed tomatoes,
drained and chopped

3 beefsteak tomatoes, peeled,
seeded, and diced

3 tablespoons olive paste

4 tablespoons chopped
fresh basil leaves

2 tablespoons chopped
fresh Italian parsley

Fine sea salt and freshly
ground black pepper

1 pound short dry maccheroncini
or fusilli

½ cup shredded pecorino cheese

1. In a skillet, heat the olive oil. Add the garlic and shallots and sauté over
medium heat until lightly golden, 2 to 3 minutes. Add the anchovies and mash
into the oil with a fork to make a fine paste. Add the capers, olives, sun-dried
tomatoes, and diced tomatoes and cook for 5 minutes over high heat. Reduce the
heat to medium, stir in the olive paste, and cook 1 minute longer, stirring occasionally. Add the basil and parsley and season with salt and pepper.

2. Cook the pasta in abundant boiling water until it is al dente; drain well.
Transfer to the skillet and toss with the sauce for 30 seconds over a high flame.
Serve with a sprinkle of shredded pecorino cheese.

SERVES 4

Trittico di pasta corta con sugo di tonno piccante

TRIO OF SHORT PASTA IN SPICY TUNA SAUCE

Mixing different pasta shapes in a single dish is a southern Italian practice that uses up leftover pasta. It is an amusing way to serve a tuna sauce with different textures of its own. It is important to select either short or long pastas but not to mix them together. Always use Italian tuna packed in olive oil, as it will enhance the flavor of this Mediterranean dish.

4 tablespoons extra-virgin olive oil

1 garlic clove, chopped

1 medium red onion, chopped

1 6-ounce can Italian tuna in olive oil, drained

½ cup dry white wine

2 beefsteak tomatoes, peeled, seeded, and cubed

1½ cups Mezzaluna Tomato Sauce (page 73)

½ teaspoon dried hot pepper

2 tablespoons chopped fresh Italian parsley

2 tablespoons chopped fresh oregano

Fine sea salt and freshly ground black pepper

6 ounces dry penne

6 ounces dry fusilli

6 ounces dry maccheroncini

1. In a skillet, heat the olive oil. Add the garlic and onion and sauté over medium heat until golden, 3 to 4 minutes. Add the tuna and wine and allow the wine to evaporate. Add the tomatoes, tomato sauce, and hot pepper and cook for 5 minutes. Add the parsley and oregano and season with salt and pepper to taste.

2. Meanwhile, cook the pastas separately in abundant boiling salted water until they are al dente, removing each variety with a skimmer or slotted spoon before adding the next. Drain well.

3. Transfer the pasta to the sauce and toss together over a high flame for 30 seconds.

SERVES 6

Maccheroncini con carciofi e rosmarino

MACCHERONCINI WITH ARTICHOKES AND ROSEMARY

This is one of my favorite recipes. In order not to detract from the flavor of the artichokes and the aroma of the rosemary, no tomato sauce is added; the delicate flavor of the artichokes is enhanced by herbs alone.

Juice of ½ lemon

8 baby artichokes

6 tablespoons extra-virgin olive oil

1 shallot, chopped

3 garlic cloves, chopped

½ cup dry white wine

1 bay leaf

1 sprig of rosemary, leaves finely chopped

Fine sea salt and freshly ground black pepper

¾ cup beef broth

1 pound dry maccheroncini

½ cup grated Parmesan cheese

2 tablespoons chopped fresh Italian parsley

1. Squeeze the half lemon into a bowl of cold water. Rinse the artichokes under running water. Remove the tough outer leaves, trim the stems, and slice the artichokes, dropping the slices into the bowl of lemon juice and water. Set aside.

2. Heat the olive oil in a skillet. Add the shallot and garlic and sauté over medium heat until golden, 3 to 4 minutes. In the meantime, drain the artichoke slices and pat them dry. Add to the skillet and mix well. Add the wine, bay leaf, and rosemary, season with salt and pepper, and cook until the wine has evaporated. Add the beef broth, lower the heat, cover, and cook for 6 minutes, until the artichoke slices are tender.

3. Meanwhile, cook the pasta in abundant boiling salted water until it is al dente. Drain well.

4. Add the pasta to the skillet and toss over high heat for 30 seconds. Top with Parmesan cheese and garnish with parsley.

SERVES 4

Fusilli con lattuga e punte di asparagi

FUSILLI WITH LETTUCE AND ASPARAGUS TIPS

Asparagus is one of my favorite vegetables. As soon as the first crop appears on the market I am reminded of my childhood and the beginning of spring.

¾ pound asparagus tips	⅔ cup dry white wine
½ cup extra-virgin olive oil, plus additional for garnish	Fine sea salt and freshly ground black pepper
2 garlic cloves, chopped	1 cup Saffron Stock (page 16)
1 large head Boston lettuce, half sliced, half cut in fine strips	1 pound dry fusilli
	½ cup grated Parmesan cheese

1. Steam the asparagus over boiling water just until they are al dente, about 5 to 7 minutes. Set aside.

2. In a skillet, heat 4 tablespoons of the olive oil. Add 1 chopped garlic clove and sauté over medium heat until lightly golden, 2 minutes. Add the sliced Boston lettuce, ⅓ cup of the white wine, and salt and pepper to taste. Cook until the wine evaporates, about 1 minute. Add the vegetable stock and continue to cook over medium heat for 3 minutes, until the lettuce has softened. Drain, place in a food processor, and chop coarsely.

3. Cook the pasta in abundant boiling salted water until it is al dente. Drain well.

4. In a skillet, heat the remaining 4 tablespoons of olive oil. Add the remaining chopped garlic clove and sauté until lightly golden, about 2 minutes. Add the lettuce strips and the remaining wine. Add the asparagus tips and the sautéed lettuce and stir well. Add the pasta to the skillet and toss over high heat for 30 seconds. Top with grated Parmesan cheese and a C of olive oil.

SERVES 4

Trofiette al mezzo pesto e fagiolini

TROFIETTE WITH HALF PESTO AND STRING BEANS

*Pesto is probably the most famous sauce of the Ligurian cuisine and
is also found along the northern riviera of the Mediterranean. Pesto
literally means "pounded" and is traditionally made in a marble mortar with
a pestle. At Mezzaluna we add some tomato to the pesto as a diluting factor
to make the dish lighter and more digestible (thus "half pesto"). In Liguria
a peeled, diced potato or two would probably be thrown in to cook with
the pasta, a hearty and pleasing addition that I recommend.*

GREEN PESTO

**2 bunches fresh basil, washed
and stems removed**

1 garlic clove, peeled

1½ tablespoons pine nuts

1 tablespoon chopped walnuts

¾ cup extra-virgin olive oil

½ cup grated Parmesan cheese

⅓ cup grated pecorino cheese

2 tablespoons extra-virgin olive oil

½ cup chopped fresh plum tomatoes

**½ cup Mezzaluna Tomato Sauce
(page 73)**

**Fine sea salt and freshly
ground black pepper**

PASTA

**2 small potatoes, peeled
and diced (optional)**

**⅓ pound haricots verts
or thin green beans, trimmed**

1 pound dry trofiette or chiocciole

**Grated pecorino cheese,
for serving**

1. In a food processor, puree the basil leaves, garlic, pine nuts, walnuts, olive oil,
Parmesan, and pecorino until you have a creamy and uniform texture. Add extra
olive oil if necessary.

2. In a skillet, heat the olive oil. Add the tomatoes and tomato sauce and cook for
2 to 3 minutes over medium heat. Season, stir in the pesto, and set aside.

3. Cook the potatoes, if using, in abundant boiling water for 7 minutes. Add the
beans and cook for 3 minutes, then add the pasta and cook together for 6 to 7
minutes until the pasta is al dente. Drain well. Transfer to the skillet and toss
over high heat for 30 seconds. Sprinkle with grated pecorino cheese.

SERVES 4

Trenette prezzemolate con vongole e olive nere

PARSLEY TRENETTE WITH CLAMS AND BLACK OLIVES

Trenette is a pasta shape made in Genoa that is most frequently served
with classic pesto sauce. I serve it with an unusual combination of clams
and olives inspired by a dish I enjoyed on the Sardinian coast.

CLAM SAUCE	PARSLEY PASTA
½ cup extra-virgin olive oil	3 eggs
3 garlic cloves, chopped	½ cup chopped fresh Italian parsley
40 Manilla clams (about 1¼ pounds) (see Note)	4 cups unbleached all-purpose flour
2 cups Mezzaluna Tomato Sauce (recipe follows)	1 tablespoon extra-virgin olive oil
¾ cup pitted Ligurian or Gaeta olives	Pinch of salt
½ cup dry white wine	3 tablespoons chopped fresh Italian parsley
Fine sea salt and freshly ground black pepper	

1. In a skillet, heat the olive oil. Add the garlic and sauté over medium heat until lightly golden, 2 to 3 minutes. Add the clams, cover, and cook over high heat for 4 to 6 minutes, until the clams have opened. Set aside and allow to cool. Transfer the clams in their shells to a bowl, reserving the cooking liquid.

2. Strain the clam cooking liquid into a saucepan. Add the tomato sauce, olives, and wine and cook over high heat for 1 minute until the wine evaporates, then cover and cook 3 minutes longer. Season with salt and pepper to taste. Set aside.

3. In a food processor, combine the eggs and parsley until well blended.

4. Pour the flour onto a large wooden board. Make a well in the center. Pour the egg and parsley mixture into the well. Add the olive oil and salt. Gradually incorporate the mixture into the dough. When all is incorporated, knead the dough until it has a smooth texture and is not wet, adding a bit more flour if needed. Shape into a ball. Roll the dough thinly with a rolling pin, then cut into ¼-inch strips.

5. Cook the trenette in abundant boiling salted water for about 3 minutes until they are al dente. Drain well.

6. Transfer the pasta to the saucepan and toss for 30 seconds over high heat. Add the clams to the pasta, removing them from the shells over the pasta so it catches the juices. Toss again, sprinkle with parsley, and serve.

SERVES 4

NOTE: Soak the clams in a bowl of cold water for at least 30 minutes, then rinse well to remove any sand.

MEZZALUNA TOMATO SAUCE

2 tablespoons extra-virgin olive oil	3 pounds ripe plum tomatoes, chopped
½ medium onion, finely chopped	1 celery stalk, finely chopped
	4 fresh basil leaves
1 garlic clove, finely chopped	Fine sea salt and freshly ground black pepper

In a skillet, heat the olive oil. Add the onion and sauté until lightly golden over medium low heat. Add the garlic, tomato, celery, and basil. Season with salt and pepper and simmer for 40 minutes. Stir often. When the sauce is cooked, use a whisk to help dissolve the tomatoes. The sauce can be kept in the refrigerator for up to 3 days, or frozen for later use.

Ravioli con zucchine e pomodori secchi

RAVIOLI WITH ZUCCHINI AND SUN-DRIED TOMATOES

My friend, Giorgio DeLuca, founder of the famous gourmet store
Dean and DeLuca, should be considered the godfather of the sun-dried tomato
in the United States. Thanks to his efforts and marketing savvy, the sun-dried
tomato has found a popularity here that far exceeds its modest appeal in Italy.
Combining the sweetness of the zucchini and the tartness of the sun-dried tomatoes
produces an interesting and unusual flavor greatly favored by our patrons.

FILLING

5 medium zucchini

4 tablespoons extra-virgin olive oil

1 shallot, chopped

2 garlic cloves, chopped

1 bay leaf

Fine sea salt and freshly
ground black pepper

2½ cups ricotta cheese,
drained in a strainer
for 30 minutes

½ cup grated Parmesan cheese

1 egg yolk

1 tablespoon chopped
fresh Italian parsley

1 recipe Basic Pasta Dough
(page 79)

SAUCE

3 tablespoons extra-virgin olive oil

2 yellow zucchini, sliced

2 green zucchini, sliced

2 garlic cloves, chopped

¾ cup chopped plum tomatoes

15 Ligurian sun-dried tomatoes,
or other oil-packed tomatoes,
drained and coarsely chopped

Fine sea salt and freshly
ground black pepper

1 tablespoon chopped fresh
Italian parsley

1. Rinse the zucchini. Cut off the ends and dice into very tiny cubes.

2. In a skillet, heat the olive oil. Add the shallot and garlic and sauté over
medium heat until lightly golden. Add the zucchini and bay leaf, raise the heat
to high, and sauté for 7 minutes, or until the zucchini is tender. Season with salt
and pepper to taste. Discard the bay leaf. Drain the zucchini and allow to cool.

3. In a bowl, combine the zucchini, the ricotta and Parmesan cheeses, the
egg yolk, and the parsley. Adjust the salt and pepper seasoning. Mix well and
set aside.

4. Roll out the pasta dough on a floured work surface or pass through a pasta machine set on the last setting. Stretch the pasta very thin, less than one-sixteenth of an inch thick. Brush the bottom layer with cold water. Stuff the ravioli by dotting half tablespoons of the filling 2 inches apart on the pasta layer. Cover with the second layer, molding the ravioli by pressing around the filling with your fingers. Cut between the rows of filling with a pasta cutter to make individual raviolis.

5. In a large skillet, heat the olive oil. Add the yellow and green zucchini and sauté on a high flame until lightly golden. Add the garlic and fresh and sun-dried tomatoes, season, and cook for 2 to 3 minutes. Add the parsley.

6. Gently cook the ravioli in abundant boiling salted water for 5 to 6 minutes, until firm but tender. Transfer with a slotted spoon or skimmer to a serving bowl and top with the sauce.

SERVES 6

Ravioli neri ai granchi

BLACK RAVIOLI WITH CRABMEAT

Colors play an important role in Mezzaluna's cuisine, and the chromatic appeal of black on black is what attracted me to experiment with this dish. Apart from the visual drama of the black ravioli, the squid ink enhances the flavor of the crabmeat and both are exquisitely complemented by our spicy tomato sauce.

4 tablespoons extra-virgin olive oil	1½ cups fresh ricotta cheese, drained
1 celery stalk, chopped	Pinch of grated nutmeg
1 carrot, peeled and finely chopped	Fine sea salt and freshly ground black pepper
1 small leek, white part only, chopped	
1 garlic clove, chopped	¼ cup bread crumbs, if necessary
1 pound fresh or canned crabmeat, picked over	1 recipe Black Pasta Dough (page 98)
1 bay leaf	1 cup Mezzaluna Tomato Sauce (page 73)
½ cup dry white wine	1 teaspoon dried hot pepper
1 tablespoon chopped fresh Italian parsley	1 teaspoon chopped fresh tarragon
	Freshly ground white pepper

1. Heat the olive oil in a large skillet. Add the celery, carrot, and leek and cook over a low flame for about 3 to 4 minutes until the vegetables are soft and lightly golden. Add the garlic and cook briefly, then stir in the crabmeat and cook for 2 minutes longer. Add the bay leaf and wine and allow it to evaporate. Add the chopped parsley, and mix well. Drain thoroughly, discarding the bay leaf, and transfer to a food processor with the ricotta and nutmeg. Season with salt and pepper and process until smooth. If the filling is too wet, gradually add some bread crumbs.

2. Divide the pasta dough in 2 pieces and roll out on a floured work surface or pass through a pasta machine set on the last setting. Stretch the pasta very thin, less than one-sixteenth of an inch thick. Brush the bottom layer with cold water. Stuff the ravioli by dotting half tablespoons of the filling 2 inches apart on the pasta layer. Cover with the second layer, pressing around the filling with your

fingers. Cut between the rows of filling with a pasta cutter to make individual raviolis.

3. Gently cook the ravioli in abundant boiling salted water for 5 to 6 minutes until firm but tender. Transfer with a slotted spoon to a serving bowl.

4. In a saucepan, heat the tomato sauce. Add the dried hot pepper and tarragon. Pour over the ravioli, sprinkle with white pepper, and serve.

SERVES 8

Strozzapreti con cipollotto e peperoncino

STROZZAPRETI WITH SPRING ONION AND CHILI PASTE

This dish reminds me of Panarea, a beautiful island off the Lipari archipelago northeast of Sicily, where I first tasted it. Its flavor is greatly complemented by the aroma and flavor of the locally grown peperoncini.

4 tablespoons extra virgin olive oil

10 scallions, white part only, chopped

2 tablespoons chopped fresh oregano

3 cups chopped plum tomatoes (about 10 tomatoes)

1 teaspoon Lipari or Szechuan chili paste

Fine sea salt and freshly ground black pepper

1 cup Saffron Stock (page 16)

1 pound dry strozzapreti or fusilli

1 tablespoon chopped fresh basil

½ cup grated Parmesan cheese

1. In a skillet, heat the olive oil. Add the scallions and sauté over medium heat until lightly golden. Add the oregano, tomatoes, and chili paste. Season with salt and pepper and cook over low heat, gradually adding the vegetable stock until the sauce is smooth and uniform.

2. Meanwhile, cook the pasta in abundant boiling salted water until it is al dente. Drain well.

3. Add the pasta to the skillet and toss for 30 seconds over high heat. Adjust the salt and pepper, add the basil, and sprinkle with Parmesan cheese.

SERVES 4

Ravioli con spinaci e ricotta

RAVIOLI WITH SPINACH AND RICOTTA

When my son Andrea was a child, we would drive to a trattoria on the
outskirts of Milano every Sunday. He became known for his obstinate predilec-
tion for these cheese-filled ravioli, ordering the same dish over and over.
I think the simplicity of the ingredients makes it a classic.

4 tablespoons extra-virgin olive oil	2 egg yolks
2 pounds fresh spinach, washed and patted dry	½ cup grated Parmesan cheese
1 garlic clove, chopped	Pinch of grated nutmeg
Fine sea salt and freshly ground black pepper	1 recipe Basic Pasta Dough (opposite)
¾ pound fresh ricotta cheese, drained in a strainer for 30 minutes	4 tablespoons (½ stick) unsalted butter
	8 whole sage leaves

1. Heat the oil in a large skillet. Add the spinach and garlic and sauté over medium heat for a few minutes until the spinach is wilted. Season with salt and pepper and set aside to cool.

2. Chop the spinach coarsely and transfer to a food processor. Add the ricotta, egg yolks, Parmesan cheese, and nutmeg and process until smooth and well blended.

3. Divide the pasta dough in 2 pieces and roll on a floured work surface or pass through a pasta machine set on the last setting. Stretch the pasta very thin, less than one-sixteenth of an inch thick. Brush one layer with cold water, then dot half tablespoons of the filling in rows 2 inches apart. Cover with the second layer, molding the ravioli by pressing around the filling with your fingers. Cut between the rows of filling with a pasta cutter to make individual raviolis.

4. Gently cook the ravioli in abundant boiling salted water for 5 to 6 minutes until firm but tender. Transfer with a slotted spoon to a serving bowl.

5. In the meantime, while you are cooking the ravioli, brown the butter in a skillet and add the sage leaves. Pour over the ravioli and serve.

SERVES 6

| 2 cups durum flour | | 3 eggs |
| 1 cup all-purpose flour | | Water as needed |

In a bowl, combine all the pasta dough ingredients and mix well until the dough is firm and dry, adding water only if necessary to make the dough come together. Cover with a damp towel and allow the dough to rest for ½ hour.

Summer

BUCATINI CON POMODORINI E QUATTRO FORMAGGI
Bucatini with cherry tomatoes and four cheeses

RIGATONI CON MELANZANE E RICOTTA SALATA
Rigatoni with eggplant and ricotta salata

FARFALLE CON CARBONARA DI VERDURE
Farfalle with carbonara of five vegetables

PENNE ALLA BISANZIO
Penne with fresh tomato, basil, and mozzarella

SPAGHETTINI CON RUCOLA E BOTTARGA
Spaghettini with arugula and sun-dried mullet roe

FUSILLI CON ZUCCHINE, MENTA, E BASILICO
Fusilli with zucchini, mint, and basil

SPAGHETTI ALLA CHITARRA ALLA CRUDAIOLA
Spaghetti alla chitarra with raw summer vegetables

GRAMIGNA CON LA PEPERONATA
Gramigna with stewed red, yellow, and green peppers

TORTIGLIONI CON FRUTTI DI MARE AL CARTOCCIO
Tortiglioni with seafood in parchment

LASAGNE CON VERDURE MISTE
Lasagne with mixed vegetables

Bucatini con pomodorini e quattro formaggi

BUCATINI WITH CHERRY TOMATOES AND FOUR CHEESES

Bucatini is a thick hollow spaghetti popular in the Lazio region. It goes well with a variety of sauces. I particularly like the combination of the four cheeses and the color and flavor of the red and yellow cherry tomatoes.

4 tablespoons extra-virgin olive oil

2 garlic cloves, chopped

3 pounds yellow and red cherry tomatoes, halved

¾ cup grated Parmesan cheese

¾ cup grated pecorino cheese

¾ cup ricotta salata cheese

¾ cup grated spicy provolone cheese

1 pound dry bucatini

12 fresh basil leaves, chopped

Fine sea salt and freshly ground black pepper

1. In a large skillet, heat the olive oil. Add the garlic and sauté over medium heat until golden, 2 to 3 minutes. Add the cherry tomatoes, lower the flame, cover, and cook gently for 20 minutes, or until they are soft.

2. In a bowl, combine the 4 cheeses. Pour half of the cheese mixture into the cooked tomatoes and cook uncovered over a low flame for a few minutes.

3. Cook the pasta in abundant boiling salted water until it is al dente. Drain well. Transfer the pasta to the sauce skillet and toss on high heat for 30 seconds. Top with the remaining cheese mixture and the basil. Season with salt and pepper to taste and serve.

SERVES 4

Rigatoni con melanzane e ricotta salata

RIGATONI WITH EGGPLANT AND RICOTTA SALATA

A typical Sicilian dish also found in other southern Italian regions, this is known in Catania as "Pasta alla Norma" in honor of that opera's famous composer, Vincenzo Bellini, who counted it among his favorite pasta fare. The eggplant, native to India and China, was most likely introduced to Italy by the Arabs, who dominated Sicily in 1200.

2 medium eggplants, cubed
1½ teaspoons salt
10 large basil leaves
6 tablespoons extra-virgin olive oil
2 garlic cloves, chopped
1 bay leaf

Fine sea salt and freshly ground black pepper
5 ripe plum tomatoes, peeled, seeded, and diced
1 pound dry rigatoni
½ cup shaved ricotta salata cheese

1. Trim the eggplants and halve lengthwise. Cut the flesh into 1-inch cubes. Place the eggplant cubes in a colander, sprinkle with the salt, and set aside for 20 minutes, or until they have released their moisture. Finely chop 6 of the basil leaves and set the rest aside for garnish.

2. In a large heavy skillet, heat 4 tablespoons of olive oil. Add the chopped garlic and sauté over medium heat until lightly golden. Add the eggplant and sauté, stirring, until golden brown, 10 to 15 minutes. Add the chopped basil and the bay leaf, season with salt and pepper, and cook for a minute or two longer. Add the tomatoes, lower the flame, and cook until they are soft and have released their liquid, 3 or 4 minutes.

3. Cook the rigatoni in abundant boiling salted water until they are al dente. Drain well and transfer to the skillet with the sauce. Add 2 tablespoons of olive oil and toss over a high flame for 30 seconds, just until heated through. Serve on individual plates, garnished with a basil leaf and some cheese shavings.

SERVES 4

TIP: To peel the tomatoes, make an incision on the skin crosswise. Place them in a bowl of hot water for a minute, then peel with your fingers.

Farfalle con carbonara di verdure

FARFALLE WITH CARBONARA OF FIVE VEGETABLES

*Carbonara is a famous old-fashioned pasta dish seasoned with a sauce
made with beaten eggs and pancetta or bacon. It was originally created in honor
of the American soldiers who liberated Italy; the combination of bacon, eggs,
and cream was meant to make them feel at home. This vegetarian interpretation
substitutes a healthy and appealing array of vegetables for the meat.*

½ pound broccoli florets	1 yellow or red bell pepper, seeded and diced
4 tablespoons extra-virgin olive oil	12 fresh basil leaves, chopped
2 garlic cloves, chopped	Fine sea salt and freshly ground black pepper
2 zucchini, trimmed and diced	2 eggs, lightly beaten
1 leek, white part only, well washed and chopped	½ cup grated Parmesan cheese
2 carrots, peeled and diced	1 pound dry farfalle

1. Blanch the broccoli florets in boiling salted water for 2 minutes. Drain and
set aside.

2. In a skillet, heat the olive oil. Add the garlic and sauté over medium heat until
lightly golden, about 2 minutes. Add the broccoli, zucchini, leek, carrots, and bell
pepper and sauté over medium heat for about 8 minutes. Add the chopped basil
and season with salt and pepper.

3. In a bowl, combine the beaten eggs with the Parmesan cheese.

4. In the meantime, bring abundant water to a boil, add salt, and cook the
farfalle until al dente. Drain well. Transfer to the skillet and toss with the vegetables over a high flame for a few seconds. Turn off the heat, stir in the eggs and
cheese until well combined, and season generously with pepper.

SERVES 4

Penne alla Bisanzio

PENNE WITH FRESH TOMATO, BASIL, AND MOZZARELLA

In this recipe, the penne is smothered in a light and colorful sauce.
Unlike traditional tomato sauces, it is cooked for only a few minutes,
so the basil and tomatoes retain their vibrant color and flavor.

1 pound dry penne	6 ounces mozzarella cheese, cubed
4 tablespoons extra-virgin olive oil	
1 pound chopped plum tomatoes	6 fresh basil leaves, chopped
3 cups Mezzaluna Tomato Sauce (page 73)	Fine sea salt and freshly ground black pepper

1. Cook the penne in abundant boiling salted water until al dente. Drain well.

2. In a skillet, heat the olive oil. Add the tomatoes and the tomato sauce and cook for 2 minutes over medium heat.

3. Add the pasta to the skillet and toss with the sauce for 30 seconds over high heat. Add the mozzarella and turn off the heat immediately. Toss again, add the basil, and adjust the seasoning with salt and pepper.

SERVES 4

NOTE: Make sure you add the mozzarella at the last minute. It should not cook, as it will become watery and chewy.

Spaghettini con rucola e bottarga

SPAGHETTINI WITH ARUGULA AND SUN-DRIED MULLET ROE

Bottarga is made from the roe of mullet that has been cured
for several hours in salt and then pressed between two pieces of wood
and allowed to sun-dry for two weeks. This gastronomic specialty is typical
of Sardinia, where mullets are particularly abundant in the northern lagoons.
Bottarga can also be made with tuna eggs, but the quality is less good. Olive
oil greatly enhances the particular flavor of the mullet roe. Together they
are a perfect condiment for pasta. I have also added a gremolata, an enticing
mix of lemon rind and parsley, which gives the dish a fine aroma.

6 tablespoons extra-virgin olive oil

2 garlic cloves, chopped

3 ounces pressed mullet roe
(*bottarga*), coarsely grated

1 pound dry spaghettini

2 bunches arugula, well washed,
stems removed

Juice of ½ lemon

2 tablespoons chopped fresh
Italian parsley

1 tablespoon grated lemon rind

Fine sea salt and freshly
ground black pepper

1. In a skillet, heat the olive oil. Add the garlic and sauté over medium heat until golden, about 2 minutes. Add the mullet roe and sauté for 30 seconds. Remove from the heat and set aside.

2. In a large pot, bring abundant water to a boil and add salt. Cook the spaghettini for 5 minutes. Add the arugula and cook until the pasta is al dente. Drain the spaghettini and arugula together and transfer to the skillet with the mullet roe. Add the lemon juice and toss over a high flame for 30 seconds. Mix the chopped parsley and grated lemon rind and sprinkle over the pasta. Season with salt and pepper to taste and serve.

SERVES 4

Fusilli con zucchine, menta, e basilico

FUSILLI WITH ZUCCHINI, MINT, AND BASIL

It was over fifteen years ago, while vacationing in Capri, that I first tasted this epicurean dish. It was a treat just to be sitting under the lemon trees of Paolino's restaurant and enjoying the beginning of spring. I was immediately captivated by the simplicity of the dish and by the richness of its flavors, the very ripe zucchini, the basil and mint, and the olive oil. At Mezzaluna, there is always great anticipation around springtime when this dish goes back on the menu. The fried zucchini adds a crisp and very appetizing dimension.

1 pound zucchini (4 or 5 medium)	1 tablespoon chopped fresh basil
All-purpose unbleached flour, for dredging	1 tablespoon chopped fresh Italian parsley
3 tablespoons extra-virgin olive oil	Fine sea salt and freshly ground black pepper
2 tablespoons unsalted butter	¼ cup corn oil
2 garlic cloves, chopped	1 pound dry fusilli
½ medium onion, chopped	1½ teaspoons chopped fresh mint
1 cup water	
1 cup grated Parmesan cheese	

1. Wash and trim the zucchini. Slice 1 zucchini into thin rounds and dredge lightly in flour. Dice the rest of the zucchini.

2. In a skillet, heat the olive oil and butter. Add the garlic and onion and sauté until lightly golden, 4 to 5 minutes. Add the diced zucchini and sauté for 1 minute over high heat. Add the water and continue to cook for 15 minutes over medium heat, until the zucchini are soft. Add ½ cup of the Parmesan cheese, the basil, and parsley. Season with salt and pepper and mix well. Set aside and keep warm.

3. In a separate skillet, heat the corn oil until very hot. Add the sliced zucchini and fry until they are golden and crispy. Remove from the oil with a skimmer and drain on a paper towel to absorb any excess oil. Keep warm.

4. Cook the pasta in abundant boiling salted water until al dente. Drain well.

Add the pasta to the skillet with the diced zucchini and toss over high heat for 30 seconds. Garnish with the fried zucchini and sprinkle with the mint and the remaining Parmesan cheese.

SERVES 4

Spaghetti alla chitarra alla crudaiola

SPAGHETTI ALLA CHITARRA WITH RAW SUMMER VEGETABLES

I think this is the perfect summer pasta dish. It is prepared with a variety of raw garden vegetables. I particularly like spaghetti alla chitarra, named for the guitarlike instrument on which it is made, for its interesting texture. Several Italian companies import dried spaghetti alla chitarra to the States; if you can't find it, substitute linguine.

8 tablespoons extra-virgin olive oil

6 ripe plum tomatoes, diced

3 celery stalks with leaves, diced

2 garlic cloves, very finely chopped

2 tablespoons finely chopped fresh Italian parsley

2 tablespoons finely chopped fresh basil leaves

1 teaspoon dried hot pepper

1 pound dry spaghetti alla chitarra

Fine sea salt and freshly ground black pepper

½ cup grated pecorino cheese

1. In a skillet, heat 4 tablespoons of the olive oil. Add the diced tomatoes and cook over high heat for 30 seconds.

2. Place the celery, garlic, parsley, basil, and hot pepper in a large bowl.

3. Cook the pasta in abundant boiling salted water until al dente. Drain well. Transfer to the skillet and toss for 30 seconds over high heat. Season with salt.

4. Add the pasta and tomatoes to the bowl with the vegetables. Add the remaining 4 tablespoons of olive oil and toss well. Sprinkle with grated pecorino cheese and season with pepper.

SERVES 4

Gramigna con la peperonata

This red, yellow, and green pepper stew originated in Emilia (the region where Bologna is), but has since found its way to other parts of Italy. It is a very gratifying dish, as much for its color as for its flavor, and the fact that the peppers are cooked for a long time makes them easy to digest. Peperonata is generally served as an appetizer or side dish with a meat course. I decided to use this particular shape of pasta because I find that it wraps up the sauce very well. I have also added some spicy provolone cheese as a counterpoint to the sweetness of the peperonata. It's a wonderful summer dish.

4 tablespoons extra-virgin olive oil

1 medium red onion, thinly sliced

2 red, 2 yellow, and 1 green bell peppers (about 1½ pounds)

2 whole garlic cloves

Fine sea salt and freshly ground black pepper

1 pound ripe plum tomatoes, chopped

1½ tablespoons chopped fresh basil

1 pound dry gramigna or ruote (wagon wheel pasta)

½ cup grated spicy provolone cheese

1. Heat the olive oil in a heavy skillet. Add the onion and cook over medium-low heat until it is very soft, 8 to 10 minutes, adding water if necessary to prevent it from sticking.

2. Wash the peppers and pat them dry. Cut in half, remove the seeds, ribs, and core, and slice in strips lengthwise.

3. Transfer the peppers to the heavy skillet. Add the garlic, season with salt and pepper, and cook for about 8 minutes over a medium flame, stirring frequently. Add the tomatoes and simmer until they begin to release their liquid. Increase the heat to medium and cook for about 30 minutes, until the peppers are very soft. Sprinkle with the basil and season with pepper.

4. Cook the pasta in abundant boiling salted water until al dente. Drain well.

5. Add the pasta to the skillet and toss for 30 seconds over high heat. Top with the spicy provolone cheese.

SERVES 4

Tortiglioni con frutti di mare al cartoccio

TORTIGLIONI WITH SEAFOOD IN PARCHMENT

Cooking seafood in a parchment wrapper keeps it moist and concentrates the flavors. Serve the pasta piping hot and break the parchment paper at the table for a dramatic release of the aromas and flavors of the sea.

6 tablespoons extra virgin olive oil	¼ pound calamari
¼ pound mussels (about 12)	½ cup dry white wine
¼ pound Manilla clams (about 18)	4 plum tomatoes, chopped
2 garlic cloves, chopped	2 tablespoons chopped fresh Italian parsley
1 teaspoon dried hot pepper	1 pound dry tortiglioni
1 shallot, chopped	Fine sea salt and freshly ground black pepper
12 medium shrimp, shelled and deveined	2 tablespoons chopped fresh basil

1. Preheat the oven to 450°F.

2. In a large saucepan, heat 2 tablespoons of the olive oil. Add the mussels and clams, cover, and cook over high heat for 2 minutes, or until they have opened. Remove the shellfish to a bowl and keep warm. Strain the liquid and reserve.

3. In the same skillet, heat the remaining 4 tablespoons of olive oil. Add the garlic, hot pepper, and shallot and sauté over low heat just until golden. Add the shrimp and calamari and cook over high heat for 2 minutes. Add the wine and cook until it has evaporated. Add the tomatoes, the reserved fish cooking liquid, and the parsley. Cook for an additional 5 minutes over medium heat.

4. Cook the pasta in abundant boiling salted water until it is very al dente. Drain well. Add the pasta, clams, and mussels to the skillet and toss together for 30 seconds over high heat. Season with salt and pepper and add the basil. Transfer the pasta and seafood to a baking sheet lined with a very large sheet of parchment paper or aluminum foil. Fold the short edges over the pasta, then fold the long edges together tightly to enclose the filling. Bake for 4 minutes.

SERVES 4

Lasagne con verdure miste

LASAGNE WITH MIXED VEGETABLES

A perfect light summer dish to make when vegetables
are at their peak, full of flavor and aroma.

1 eggplant

2 zucchini

1 red bell pepper,
seeded and chopped

1 yellow bell pepper,
seeded and chopped

1 garlic clove, finely chopped

1 cup chiffonade of fresh basil
(see Note)

Fine sea salt and freshly
ground black pepper

⅔ cup extra-virgin olive oil

½ cup chopped fresh
shiitake mushrooms

4 Fresh Lasagna Sheets, homemade
(recipe follows) or purchased
(approximately ¾ pound)

3 cups Béchamel Sauce
(page 117)

1 tablespoon butter

2 beefsteak tomatoes, peeled,
seeded, and cubed

¾ cup Mezzaluna Tomato Sauce
(page 73)

2 cups grated Parmesan cheese

1. Peel and trim the eggplant. Cut lengthwise into ½-inch slices. Trim the zucchini and cut into ¼-inch rounds. In a large bowl, combine the eggplant, zucchini, peppers, garlic, ½ cup of the basil chiffonade, salt and pepper, and ½ cup of the olive oil, and marinate for 2 to 3 hours at room temperature.

2. Grill the vegetables on a stovetop grill pan, charcoal grill, or broiler until tender; set aside.

3. In a skillet, heat 2 tablespoons of olive oil. Add the mushrooms and sauté over medium heat for 3 minutes. Set aside.

4. Parboil each lasagna sheet in abundant boiling salted water for 2 minutes. Retrieve with a skimmer and rinse under cold running water. Spread the sheets on a dry kitchen towel and brush both sides with olive oil to prevent sticking.

5. Preheat the oven to 350°F.

6. Pour 1 cup of béchamel sauce over the bottom of a buttered 13 × 8 × 2-inch lasagne pan and arrange about a quarter of the grilled vegetables on top. Add a pasta sheet, cover with a quarter of the grilled vegetables, add some mushrooms, some diced tomatoes, 4 tablespoons of tomato sauce, ½ cup béchamel sauce, some of the remaining basil chiffonade, and ½ cup Parmesan cheese. Repeat the procedure 2 times, ending with Parmesan cheese, ½ cup béchamel, and the remaining tomato sauce. Bake for 25 minutes, until the lasagne is bubbling and golden brown.

SERVES 6

NOTE: To make the basil chiffonade, stack the basil leaves and cut into very fine strips.

FRESH LASAGNA SHEETS

4 cups unbleached all-purpose flour	**1 tablespoon extra-virgin olive oil**
3 eggs, lightly beaten	**Water as needed**
Salt	

1. On a large work surface or cutting board, pour the flour into a mound and make a well in the center. Pour the eggs, salt, and olive oil in the well. Using your hands, work the ingredients gradually together until you have a smooth dough, adding a small amount of water if the dough is too stiff. Knead briefly (about 10 minutes), then flatten the dough in the shape of a rectangle about ⅛ inch thick. Set aside between sheets of wax paper or place in a plastic bag to prevent it from drying out until ready to roll.

2. Divide the pasta into 4 equal portions and with a rolling pin or pasta machine roll each into a thin (⅜-inch) sheet approximately 8 × 12 inches. Allow to dry on the counter for 2 or 3 minutes.

MAKES 1½ POUNDS

Autumn

MALTAGLIATI VERDI CON RADICCHIO E PANCETTA
Spinach maltagliati with radicchio and pancetta

CAVATELLI CON PESTO DI RUCOLA E PATATE
Cavatelli with arugula pesto and potatoes

SEDANI CON CAVOLFIORI
Sedani with cauliflower

TUBETTINI CON PROSCIUTTO, PISELLI, E FONTINA
Tubettini with prosciutto, peas, and fontina cheese

PENNETTE CON ZUCCA E RICOTTA AFFUMICATA
Pennette with pumpkin and smoked ricotta

LINGUINE NERE SCIUE SCIUE
Black linguine in spicy tomato sauce

CANNELLONI ALLA SORRENTINA
Cannelloni Sorrento style

MACCHERONCELLI AL FORNO ALLA VESUVIO
Baked maccheroncelli with mozzarella and spicy tomato sauce

LASAGNE CON RADICCHIO E FUNGHI
Radicchio and wild mushroom lasagne

PAPPARDELLE CON FUNGHI PORCINI E TARTUFI
Pappardelle with porcini mushrooms and truffles

Maltagliati verdi con radicchio e pancetta

*Maltagliati or "badly cut" pasta are irregular-shaped pasta scraps.
I prefer spinach maltagliati for its texture and for its color, which complements
the purple radicchio; however, you may substitute dried fusilli if you wish.*

SPINACH PASTA

¼ cup cooked spinach, lightly steamed or thawed frozen

3 eggs

4 cups all-purpose flour

4 tablespoons extra-virgin olive oil

2 garlic cloves, chopped

4 ounces pancetta or slab bacon, cubed

2 medium heads radicchio, coarsely chopped

⅓ cup dry white wine

1½ cups Mezzaluna Tomato Sauce (page 73)

Fine sea salt and freshly ground black pepper

½ cup grated Parmesan cheese

1. Squeeze as much moisture as possible from the spinach. Combine with the eggs in a blender or food processor and puree until the spinach is finely chopped. Place the flour in a bowl and make a well in the top. Pour the egg-spinach mixture into the well and, using your hands, gradually incorporate into the flour to make a smooth dough. If the dough is too sticky, add flour. Turn the dough onto a work surface and knead until very smooth, about 10 minutes.

2. Roll the dough to ¹⁄₁₆ inch thick, then use a sharp knife to cut the pasta into irregularly shaped diamond pieces approximately 1¼ inches in diameter.

3. In a skillet, heat the olive oil. Add the garlic and sauté over medium heat until lightly golden. Add the pancetta and cook until the fat begins to render. Add the radicchio and cook for 5 minutes. Drain off the excess fat, add the wine, and cook until it has evaporated. Add the tomato sauce and cook for 5 minutes.

4. Cook the pasta in abundant boiling salted water until it is al dente. Drain well and add to the skillet with the sauce. Toss over high heat for 30 seconds. Season with salt and pepper, sprinkle with the Parmesan cheese, and serve.

SERVES 4

Cavatelli con pesto di rucola e patate

CAVATELLI WITH ARUGULA PESTO AND POTATOES

*Here the flavor of arugula is intensified by the addition of an
arugula pesto, which also gives the dish an appealing texture.*

3 bunches arugula

2 Yukon gold potatoes

1 fresh sage leaf

Extra-virgin olive oil

1 garlic clove, peeled

2 tablespoons pine nuts

1 cup grated Parmesan cheese,
plus extra for garnish

Fine sea salt and freshly
ground black pepper

1 pound dry cavatelli or orecchiete

1 plum tomato, diced,
for garnish (optional)

1. Rinse the arugula thoroughly. Remove the stems and pat dry. Blanch
2 arugula bunches for 1 minute in boiling salted water. Rinse in cold water
and drain well. Shred the remaining bunch of arugula and set aside.

2. Peel and dice the potatoes. Cook in salted water to cover with the sage leaf
and 1 teaspoon of olive oil until tender, 10 to 12 minutes. Drain and set aside.

3. In a food processor, combine the garlic, blanched arugula, pine nuts, and
3 tablespoons of olive oil. Process until it is smooth but not liquid. Add the grated
Parmesan cheese, season with salt and pepper, and mix well.

4. Cook the pasta in abundant boiling salted water until it is al dente.
Drain well.

5. Transfer the pasta to a skillet. Add the arugula pesto, shredded arugula, the
potatoes, and a touch of olive oil. Toss together over high heat for 30 seconds.
Sprinkle with Parmesan cheese and season with pepper. Garnish with the diced
tomato, if desired.

SERVES 4

Sedani con cavolfiore

SEDANI WITH CAULIFLOWER

I have added raisins to a traditional recipe from the Apulia
region, giving it both sweetness and contrast.

1 pound cauliflower, broken into small florets	**⅓ cup raisins, soaked in warm water and drained**
4 tablespoons extra-virgin olive oil	**Fine sea salt and freshly ground black pepper**
2 Italian anchovy fillets, packed in olive oil	**1 pound dry sedani or penne**
2 scallions, white and green parts, chopped	**½ cup toasted bread crumbs**
½ cup pitted black olives	**½ cup grated provolone cheese**

1. Soak the cauliflower florets in a large bowl of cold water for 15 minutes. Drain. Cook the florets in abundant boiling salted water for 7 minutes over medium heat.

2. Combine the olive oil and anchovies in a skillet. Cook over low heat, stirring the anchovies with a fork until they dissolve into the oil. Add the scallions and sauté until lightly golden over a medium flame. Add the cauliflower, olives, and raisins and sauté for 3 to 4 minutes. Season with salt and pepper to taste.

3. Cook the pasta in abundant boiling salted water until al dente. Drain well.

4. Transfer the pasta to the skillet and toss for 30 seconds over high heat. Top with the toasted bread crumbs and the grated provolone cheese.

SERVES 4

Tubettini con prosciutto, piselli, e fontina

TUBETTINI WITH PROSCIUTTO, PEAS, AND FONTINA CHEESE

This is a typical southern Italian dish that should be eaten with a spoon.
I have substituted fontina cheese, with its sweeter taste, for the traditional provolone.
The tiny shape of the pasta mixes perfectly with peas, prosciutto, and cheese.

2 tablespoons extra-virgin olive oil	1 bay leaf
2 tablespoons (¼ stick) unsalted butter	2 cups Saffron Stock (page 16)
1 shallot, chopped	Fine sea salt and freshly ground black pepper
1 garlic clove, chopped	1 pound dry tubettini
½ cup prosciutto, cut into fine strips (about 10 ounces)	1 cup cubed fontina cheese
	½ cup grated Parmesan cheese
2½ cups fresh green peas or 1 10-ounce package frozen tiny peas, thawed	1 tablespoon chopped fresh Italian parsley

1. In a skillet, heat the olive oil and butter. Add the shallot and garlic and sauté over a medium flame until golden, 3 to 4 minutes. Add the prosciutto and cook for 2 minutes, then add the peas, bay leaf, vegetable stock, and salt and pepper. Mix well and continue to cook for 30 minutes, until the peas are soft and creamy, adding more broth if necessary.

2. Meanwhile, cook the pasta in abundant boiling salted water until it is al dente. Drain well.

3. Return the pasta to the pot you cooked it in. Add the sauce and the cubed fontina, turn the heat to high, and toss with wooden spoons for 30 seconds. Top with the grated Parmesan cheese and the parsley. Season with salt and pepper.

SERVES 4

Pennette con zucca e ricotta affumicata

PENNETTE WITH PUMPKIN AND SMOKED RICOTTA

*In my childhood, my grandmother prepared this dish for me and it was always
one of my favorites. The flavor of Italian pumpkin (zucca) is quite different from its
American counterpart, with a spicy sweetness and a softer texture. Lynne Rossetto
Kasper, in her wonderful book* The Splendid Table, *recommends blending butternut
squash and some sweet potato in order to approximate the flavor of zucca.*

One 1¼ pound pumpkin (to yield ¾ pound, peeled and seeded) or a mix of butternut squash and sweet potatoes

4 crushed amaretti cookies

1 tablespoon unsalted butter

Pinch of nutmeg

4 tablespoons extra-virgin olive oil

1 scallion, chopped

1 garlic clove, chopped

½ teaspoon dried hot pepper

1 cup water or Saffron Stock (page 16)

1 tablespoon chopped fresh Italian parsley

1 pound dry pennette

2 tablespoons heavy cream

Fine sea salt and freshly ground black pepper

½ cup shredded smoked ricotta or ricotta salata

1. Preheat the oven to 350° F.

2. Cut two-thirds of the pumpkin (about ½ pound) into ¼-inch slices; cube the
rest and set aside. Place the pumpkin slices on a greased baking sheet and bake
for 40 minutes. Pass through a food mill or ricer and place the puree in a bowl
with the amaretti cookies, butter, and nutmeg. Mix well.

3. In a skillet, heat the olive oil. Add the scallion, garlic, and hot pepper and
sauté over medium heat until lightly golden, 2 or 3 minutes. Add the cubed
pumpkin and sauté for a few minutes. Add the water or vegetable stock and
parsley, reduce the heat to low, and continue to cook for 20 minutes, stirring often.

4. Cook the pasta in abundant boiling salted water until al dente. Drain well.

5. Add the pumpkin puree to the sauce, then stir in the heavy cream. Add the
pasta and toss over high heat for 30 seconds. Season with salt and pepper.
Sprinkle the shredded cheese over the dish and serve.

SERVES 4

Linguine nere sciue sciue

BLACK LINGUINE IN SPICY TOMATO SAUCE

Sciue sciue in Neapolitan dialect means "easy come, easy go."
Indeed, always in high demand at Mezzaluna, this very simple recipe
of black pasta in deep red spicy sauce tastes as dramatic as it looks.

BLACK PASTA DOUGH	SPICY TOMATO SAUCE
4 cups sifted unbleached all-purpose flour	**2 tablespoons extra-virgin olive oil**
2 tablespoons water	**1 garlic clove, chopped**
1 tablespoon squid ink	**1 teaspoon dried hot pepper**
1 tablespoon olive oil	**2 beefsteak tomatoes, peeled, seeded, and finely chopped**
3 eggs	**1 cup Mezzaluna Tomato Sauce (page 73)**
Dash of salt	
	Chopped fresh Italian parsley, for garnish

1. Make the pasta dough: Place the flour in a mound in the center of a work surface or cutting board. With a spoon, make a depression in the center of the mound.

2. In a bowl, combine the water, squid ink, olive oil, eggs, and salt. Pour the egg mixture into the depression and, with a fork, gradually draw the flour into the mixture. When it is well incorporated, knead the dough until you have a smooth mixture and the dough is not wet, adding more flour if needed. Shape into a ball.

3. Roll the dough very thinly (one eighth of an inch thick) with a rolling pin and cut into very thin strips using a very sharp knife. (If you are using a pasta machine, choose the linguine setting.) Set aside on a lightly floured cotton towel or pasta rack to dry slightly.

4. Make the Spicy Tomato Sauce: In a skillet, heat the olive oil. Add the chopped garlic and sauté until lightly golden, a minute or two. Add the hot pepper and tomatoes and cook for 1 minute. Add the tomato sauce, reduce the heat, and simmer for 5 minutes.

5. Cook the linguine in abundant salted water until al dente. Drain well. Add the pasta to the skillet and toss over high heat for 30 seconds. Top with a generous sprinkle of chopped fresh parsley and serve immediately.

SERVES 4

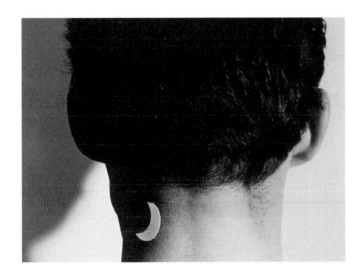

Cannelloni alla Sorrentina

CANNELLONI SORRENTO STYLE

*Depending on the stuffing and seasonings, cannelloni can be either an
elaborate preparation or a last-minute family meal. For a heartier version, replace
the tomato sauce with an equal amount of Bolognese Sauce (page 116).*

1 tablespoon unsalted butter	¼ pound fresh ricotta cheese, drained
2 tablespoons extra-virgin olive oil	2 ounces prosciutto, finely chopped
½ pound ground beef round	4 Fresh Lasagna Sheets, homemade (page 91) or purchased (approximately ¾ pound)
3 eggs	
¾ cup grated Parmesan cheese	½ cup Béchamel Sauce (page 117)
¾ pound mozzarella cheese, finely diced	¾ cup Mezzaluna Tomato Sauce (page 73)

1. In a skillet, heat the butter and olive oil. Add the beef and sauté for 5 minutes over medium heat, pressing it occasionally with a fork to break up and brown evenly. Drain off the fat.

2. In a bowl, beat the eggs and gradually add ¼ cup Parmesan cheese. Add the mozzarella, the ricotta, the prosciutto, and the ground beef. Mix well.

3. Cut the pasta sheets into 4 × 5-inch rectangles. Allow the rectangles to dry for 2 minutes, then cook in abundant gently boiling salted water, 2 sheets at a time, for about 2 minutes. Retrieve with a skimmer-drainer and rinse under cold running water. Transfer onto a wet cotton kitchen towel. Spread about 5 tablespoons of the stuffing along one long edge of each pasta rectangle. Beginning at the edge with the stuffing, roll the cannelloni loosely over the filling. Repeat with the remaining pasta and filling.

4. Preheat the oven to 350°F.

5. Place the cannelloni seam side up in a buttered 13 × 8 × 2-inch baking dish. Cover with the béchamel sauce, top with tomato sauce, and sprinkle with the remaining Parmesan cheese. Bake for 20 minutes, until bubbling and golden.

SERVES 8

Maccheroncelli al forno alla Vesuvio

BAKED MACCHERONCELLI WITH MOZZARELLA

AND SPICY TOMATO SAUCE

I have always been a great lover of pasta al forno, *"baked pasta," because
you can prepare it ahead of time and you can also store it in the freezer. Most
important, you can make a superb pasta dish in almost no time at all. Our version
of "Vesuvio" has some hot red pepper to give it a vibrant spiciness; it's my own
interpretation of this classic of the Neapolitan cuisine that's been a great success
at Mezzaluna. Serve it piping hot with a sprinkle of Parmesan cheese and pepper.*

1 pound dry maccheroncelli	6 ounces mozzarella cheese, diced
2 cups Mezzaluna Tomato Sauce (page 73)	1 cup Béchamel Sauce (page 117)
2 teaspoons dried hot pepper	1 cup grated sharp pecorino cheese
1 tablespoon chopped fresh oregano	2 tablespoons ($\frac{1}{4}$ stick) unsalted butter
Fine sea salt and freshly ground black pepper	

1. Preheat the oven to 350° F.

2. Cook the pasta in abundant boiling salted water until it is very al dente,
about 7 to 8 minutes. Do not overcook; the pasta will cook further as it bakes.
Drain well.

3. Transfer the pasta to a skillet. Add the tomato sauce, hot pepper, and oregano.
Season with salt and pepper to taste. Sauté for a minute or two over high heat.
Stir in the mozzarella.

4. Transfer the pasta to a buttered rectangular baking dish. Stir in the béchamel
sauce and top with the pecorino cheese. Bake for 15 minutes, until golden
and bubbling.

SERVES 4

Lasagne con radicchio e funghi

RADICCHIO AND WILD MUSHROOM LASAGNE

Each year the town of Treviso holds a radicchio festival. In 1992, the weeklong
festivities in this community near Venice prompted my friend Francesco Antonucci,
chef and owner of Remi in New York, to join in the revelry with a feast of his own.
Among his special guests was the celebrated chef of Treviso's Celeste restaurant. I was
lucky enough to be there and taste this delightful dish, which combines the bitter flavor
of radicchio with the heartiness of mushrooms in a very appealing way. I have added
the fontina melt to give it extra texture. It is the perfect dish to enjoy by a fireplace.

4 medium heads radicchio

1 tablespoon unsalted butter

5 tablespoons extra-virgin olive oil

1 scallion, chopped

1 garlic clove

1 tablespoon chopped fresh Italian parsley

1 pound fresh shiitake mushrooms, stems removed, sliced

Fine sea salt and freshly ground black pepper

4 Fresh Lasagna Sheets, homemade (page 91) or purchased (approximately ¾ pound)

FONTINA MELT

6 cups milk

¾ cup (1½ sticks) unsalted butter

1 cup all-purpose flour

1 pound fontina cheese, diced

Pinch of grated nutmeg

3 ripe plum tomatoes, finely diced

2 tablespoons chopped fresh basil

2 cups grated Parmesan cheese

1. Preheat the oven to 350° F.

2. Trim and rinse the radicchio and chop coarsely.

3. In a skillet, heat the butter and 3 tablespoons of oil. Add the radicchio and
scallion and sauté for 2 or 3 minutes over medium-high heat. Set aside.

4. In another skillet, heat the remaining 2 tablespoons of oil. Add the garlic and
parsley and sauté for 2 to 3 minutes over medium-low heat. Add the mushrooms,
season with salt and pepper, and sauté for 10 minutes over medium heat.

5. Parboil each lasagna sheet in abundant boiling salted water for 2 minutes.

Retrieve with a skimmer and rinse in cold water. Spread the sheets on a dry kitchen towel and brush both sides with olive oil to prevent sticking.

6. In a saucepan, bring the milk just to a boil, then remove from the heat and set aside. In another saucepan, melt the butter over low heat. Add the flour gradually, whisking constantly for 2 to 3 minutes until it is well blended. Add the hot milk, mix well, and continue to cook over a high flame for 3 minutes, until thickened. Add the diced fontina and simmer over a low flame for 15 minutes, stirring continuously, until very creamy and smooth. Add a pinch of nutmeg.

7. Pour 1 cup of fontina melt over the bottom of a 13 × 8 × 2-inch lasagne pan and cover with some of the radicchio and mushrooms. Add a sheet of pasta and top with 1 cup of fontina melt and another layer of mushrooms and radicchio. Sprinkle with some diced tomatoes, some chopped basil, and ½ cup grated Parmesan cheese. Repeat this procedure 2 times, ending with another layer of pasta. Top the lasagne with a final cup of fontina melt and more grated Parmesan.

8. Bake the lasagne for 20 minutes, until it is bubbling and golden brown.

SERVES 6

Pappardelle con funghi porcini e tartufi

PAPPARDELLE WITH PORCINI MUSHROOMS AND TRUFFLES

Pappardelle is a flat noodle that pairs particularly well with mushrooms. This is a traditional Italian recipe typical to the Piedmont, Emilia, and other northern Italian regions, where the majority of porcini mushrooms are harvested.

3 ounces dried porcini mushrooms	**1 pound fresh pappardelle (see Note)**
2 cups lukewarm water	**2 tablespoons (¼ stick) unsalted butter**
½ cup olive oil	**3 tablespoons black truffle paste**
1 garlic clove, chopped	**½ cup chopped fresh Italian parsley**
2 shallots, chopped	**Fine sea salt and freshly ground black pepper**
½ pound fresh porcini or fresh shiitake mushrooms, chopped	

1. Soak the dried porcini mushrooms in the warm water for 2 hours. Drain, strain the soaking liquid, and reserve separately.

2. In a skillet, heat the olive oil over medium heat. Add the chopped garlic and shallots and cook until lightly golden, 1 or 2 minutes. Add the fresh and dried mushrooms, then gradually add the reserved liquid. Bring to a simmer and cook for about 20 to 25 minutes.

3. Cook the pappardelle in abundant boiling salted water until al dente, about 3 to 4 minutes. Drain well.

4. Add the pasta to the skillet. Add the butter, truffle paste, and parsley and toss over a high flame for 30 seconds, until heated through. Season with salt and pepper and serve.

SERVES 4

NOTE: If you would like to make your own pappardelle, use the Basic Pasta Dough recipe on page 79; roll out very thin—one sixteenth of an inch—and cut into 2-inch-wide strips with a pastry wheel. Purchased pasta sheets are also acceptable for pappardelle; cut as above.

Winter

CONCHIGLIE CON COTECHINO E LENTICCHIE
Shells with cotechino sausage and lentils

TAGLIOLINI CON GAMBERETTI E RADICCHIO
Tagliolini with shrimp and radicchio

SPAGHETTI CON POMODORI AL FORNO, PEPOLINO, E PECORINO PEPATO
Spaghetti with oven-roasted tomatoes, thyme, and peppered pecorino

ORECCHIETTE CON CIME DI RAPA E SALSICCIA
Orecchiette with broccoli rabe and sweet sausage

FARFALLE ALLE BARBABIETOLE ROSSE
Farfalle with red beet sauce

MALLOREDDU CON SALSICCIA PICCANTE
Malloreddu with spicy sausage in tomato sauce

GNOCCHI DI PATATE DOLCI CON SALSA DI CIME DI RAPA
Sweet potato gnocchi with broccoli rabe sauce

LASAGNE VERDI BOLOGNESE
Green lasagne with Bolognese sauce

TORTELLI DI ZUCCA CON SALSA ROSA
Pumpkin tortelli with pink sauce

RAVIOLI CON PORCINI E TARTUFI
Ravioli with porcini mushrooms and truffles

Conchiglie con cotechino e lenticchie

SHELLS WITH COTECHINO SAUSAGE AND LENTILS

The shape of the conchiglie works especially well with this
unusual combination of sausage and lentils, which in Italy is generally
eaten as a main course during New Year's festivities.

1 pound cotechino sausage	Fine sea salt and freshly ground black pepper
1 small onion, very finely sliced	½ cup cooked lentils
7 tablespoons extra-virgin olive oil	½ tablespoon chopped fresh Italian parsley
½ cup Saffron Stock (page 16)	
½ pound plum tomatoes, diced	1 pound dry conchiglie
2 fresh sage leaves, chopped	½ cup grated Parmesan cheese
1 sprig of thyme	

1. Soak the cotechino sausage in warm water for 1 hour. Drain, pierce in several places with a fork, and transfer to a saucepan with water to cover. Bring to a boil and cook for 1½ hours. Leave in the hot water until ready to use.

2. In a skillet, combine the onion, 3 tablespoons of olive oil, and 3 tablespoons of vegetable stock. Bring to a simmer, then cover and cook over low heat for 7 to 8 minutes.

3. Add the tomatoes. Raise the heat to high and cook for 3 to 4 minutes. Add 1 chopped sage leaf and ½ thyme sprig. Season with salt and pepper.

4. Remove the skin from the cotechino sausage and roughly chop the meat into small pieces. Add to the tomato sauce and cook for 10 minutes over medium heat. Add the lentils, lower the flame, and simmer for a few minutes, adding the remaining vegetable stock if the sauce becomes too thick. Season with the parsley and add the remaining sage, thyme, and olive oil.

5. Meanwhile, cook the pasta in abundant boiling salted water until al dente. Drain well.

6. Add the pasta to the skillet and toss over high heat for 30 seconds. Sprinkle with the Parmesan cheese and black pepper.

SERVES 4

Tagliolini con gamberetti e radicchio

TAGLIOLINI WITH SHRIMP AND RADICCHIO

*In this dish the slightly bitter tang of radicchio is the counterpoint
to the sweetness of shrimp. It is a marriage of land and sea ingredients that
can also be used to prepare a risotto typical of the Venetian region.*

2 tablespoons (¼ stick) unsalted butter	¼ cup extra-virgin olive oil
2 shallots, finely chopped	2 garlic cloves, chopped
1 pound medium shrimp (about 32), peeled and deveined	2 heads radicchio, shredded
Fine sea salt and freshly ground black pepper	½ cup dry white wine
2 tablespoons dry sherry	2½ cups chopped plum tomatoes
	1 pound fresh tagliolini

1. In a skillet, heat the butter. Add the shallots and sauté over medium heat until golden, 2 or 3 minutes. Lower the flame, add the shrimp, season with salt and pepper, and cook, stirring occasionally, until they turn orange on both sides, about 1 to 2 minutes. Add the sherry and continue to cook until it evaporates. Set aside and keep warm.

2. In a large saucepan, heat the olive oil. Add the garlic and sauté over low heat until lightly golden, 3 to 4 minutes. Add the radicchio and sauté for a few minutes, until wilted. Raise the heat, add the white wine, and allow it to evaporate; then add the tomatoes and cook for 5 minutes. Season with salt and pepper.

3. Cook the pasta in abundant boiling salted water until it is al dente. Drain well. Transfer the tagliolini to the skillet with the shrimp and toss with the sauce over high heat for a few seconds. Adjust the seasoning with salt and pepper.

SERVES 4

Spaghetti con pomodori al forno, pepolino, e pecorino pepato

SPAGHETTI WITH OVEN-ROASTED TOMATOES, THYME,

AND PEPPERED PECORINO

This is a very simple but extremely flavorful recipe, which can be prepared in a number of different ways. The common denominator is the fresh thyme, which plays a fundamental role in blending the tomatoes with the peppery spicy taste of the pecorino cheese. In the wintertime I use oven-roasted tomatoes because they are more savory, but during the summer months, when tomatoes are at their peak, try this with fresh beefsteak tomatoes.

3 pounds ripe plum tomatoes, halved	10 fresh basil leaves, chopped
½ tablespoon chopped fresh rosemary	Fine sea salt and freshly ground black pepper
3 tablespoons chopped fresh thyme	1 pound dry spaghetti
1½ teaspoons sugar	1 cup shaved peppered pecorino cheese, or regular pecorino plus 1 teaspoon ground black pepper
3 garlic cloves	
4 tablespoons extra-virgin olive oil	

1. Preheat the oven to 300° F.

2. To make the oven-roasted tomatoes: Place the plum tomatoes on a baking sheet, cut sides up. Sprinkle with the rosemary, 1 tablespoon of thyme, and the sugar. Chop 2 garlic cloves finely and sprinkle over the tomatoes. Bake for 3 hours. Allow the tomatoes to cool, then peel, seed, and chop them.

3. Heat the olive oil in a skillet. Add the remaining whole garlic clove and sauté until lightly golden, 1 or 2 minutes. Add the oven-roasted tomatoes and the basil leaves and cook for 2 to 3 minutes over medium heat. Adjust the seasoning with salt and pepper to taste.

4. Cook the pasta in abundant boiling salted water until it is al dente. Drain well.

5. Transfer the pasta to the skillet and add the remaining 2 tablespoons of thyme and the pecorino cheese. Toss over high heat for 30 seconds.

SERVES 4

Orecchiette con cime di rapa e salsiccia

ORECCHIETTE WITH BROCCOLI RABE AND SWEET SAUSAGE

To the housewives of Apulia, making orecchiete is a joyful and social
ritual. The durum wheat pasta is shaped by hand by applying pressure with
the thumbs and then is left to dry for a day or so. The shape of this pasta
is typical of southern Italy. Combining it with cime di rapa *is a classic. I have*
added some fresh ginger at the end to enhance the flavor of the broccoli rabe,
just as the ancient Romans did, according to the food critic Apicius.

1 bunch broccoli rabe	**2 garlic cloves, chopped**
½ pound sweet Italian sausage, skins removed	**1 tablespoon grated fresh ginger**
½ cup dry white wine	**Fine sea salt and freshly ground black pepper**
2 cups Mezzaluna Tomato Sauce (page 73)	**1 pound dry orecchiette**
¼ cup extra-virgin olive oil	**½ cup grated pecorino cheese**
½ teaspoon dried hot pepper	

1. Cook the broccoli rabe in abundant boiling salted water for 3 to 5 minutes, until it is tender. Drain well. Chop coarsely and set aside.

2. In a large skillet, sauté the sausage over medium heat for a few minutes. Drain the excess fat and water. Add the wine and allow it to evaporate. Add the tomato sauce and simmer for 15 minutes.

3. In the meantime, in a separate pan, heat the olive oil. Add the broccoli rabe, hot pepper, and garlic and sauté on medium-high heat for a few minutes. Add the ginger. Transfer to the sauce and mix well. Season with salt and pepper.

4. Cook the pasta in abundant boiling salted water until it is al dente. Drain well. Toss in the sauce over high heat for 30 seconds. Sprinkle with pecorino cheese.

SERVES 4

Farfalle alle barbabietole rosse

FARFALLE WITH RED BEET SAUCE

This is a very colorful dish created by my friend Umberto Montano, owner of Le Murate restaurant in Florence. I consider it an Italian country-style version of sweet and sour. Canned beets can certainly be used, although oven-roasted beets are sweeter.

5 tablespoons extra-virgin olive oil

1 small red onion, chopped

½ cup dry white wine

12 ounces red beets, cooked, peeled, and diced (see Note)

2 ounces soft goat cheese

2 tablespoons (¼ stick) unsalted butter

1 tablespoon heavy cream

1 pound dry farfalle

Fine sea salt and freshly ground black pepper

½ cup grated Parmesan cheese

12 fresh basil leaves, chopped

1. Heat the olive oil in a skillet. Add the onion and sauté over medium heat until golden brown, about 6 to 8 minutes. Add the wine and allow it to evaporate. Add the beets and sauté for a few minutes.

2. In a food processor, puree the beets and onion, the goat cheese, 1 tablespoon of butter, and the heavy cream until the texture is uniform.

3. Cook the pasta in abundant boiling salted water until it is al dente. Drain well.

4. In a skillet, melt the remaining tablespoon of butter over medium heat. Sauté the pureed beet mixture for 3 minutes. Add the farfalle and toss for 15 seconds over a high flame. Season with salt and pepper.

5. Sprinkle with the Parmesan cheese and basil, season with freshly ground pepper, and serve.

SERVES 4

NOTE: To roast beets, individually wrap unpeeled beets in aluminum foil. Place on a baking sheet and roast at 350° F. for 40 to 50 minutes, or until they can be pierced easily with the point of a sharp knife. Cool briefly, then slip off the skins.

Malloreddu con salsiccia piccante

MALLOREDDU WITH SPICY SAUSAGE IN TOMATO SAUCE

A Sardinian specialty, malloreddu *means "little veals" in the local dialect. Their shapes look like tiny dumplings. I particularly like the saffron-flavored malloreddu, available in Italian specialty stores.*

4 tablespoons extra-virgin olive oil	3 cups chopped plum tomatoes (about 1¼ pounds)
2 shallots, chopped	½ cup beef broth
1 celery stalk, chopped	1 pound dry malloreddu
2 garlic cloves, chopped	1 tablespoon chopped fresh Italian parsley
¾ pound spicy Italian sausage, casings removed	Fine sea salt and freshly ground black pepper
½ cup dry white wine	

1. Heat the olive oil in a skillet. Add the shallots, celery, and garlic and sauté for a few minutes over medium heat until softened. In the meantime, in another pan, sauté the sausage for 2 to 3 minutes, breaking it up with a fork. Drain off the fat and add the sausage to the softened vegetables. Cook together for 2 to 3 minutes, then add the wine and allow it to evaporate. Add the tomatoes and cook for 30 minutes over medium heat, adding some of the beef broth to dilute the sauce if it becomes too thick.

2. Cook the pasta in abundant boiling salted water until it is al dente. Drain well. Add the drained pasta to the sauce and toss over high heat for a few seconds.

3. Sprinkle with the chopped parsley, season with salt and pepper to taste, and serve.

SERVES 4

Gnocchi di patate dolci con salsa di cime di rapa

SWEET POTATO GNOCCHI WITH BROCCOLI RABE SAUCE

Until the 1700s, gnocchi were made with flour and water. When the potato was introduced from the New World it became the primary ingredient of gnocchi. This version uses sweet potatoes, which balance the bitter taste of the broccoli rabe.

6 sweet potatoes, cut in quarters	2¼ pounds broccoli rabe
3 cups unbleached all-purpose flour	4 tablespoons extra-virgin olive oil
2 egg yolks	1 garlic clove, chopped
½ cup grated Parmesan cheese	1 Italian anchovy fillet, packed in olive oil
Fine sea salt and freshly ground black pepper	1 cup water
Pinch of nutmeg	½ cup shaved pecorino cheese

1. Boil the potatoes in lightly salted water until they are very tender, 12 to 14 minutes. Drain, peel, and pass through a food mill or ricer; do not puree in a food processor as the texture will be too gummy. Place the puree in a mixing bowl with the flour, egg yolks, Parmesan cheese, salt and pepper, and nutmeg and mix well. With your hands, form the dough into gnocchi about the size and shape of large olives, spreading them on a lightly floured cotton kitchen towel. Set aside.

2. Separate the broccoli rabe flowers from the stems. Chop the stems.

3. In a pan, heat the olive oil. Add the garlic and sauté over medium heat until golden, 1 or 2 minutes. Add the anchovy, lower the flame, and dissolve it with a fork into a fine paste. Add the water and the broccoli stems, season with salt and pepper, and cook uncovered over a medium flame for about 20 minutes, adding water if necessary, until the broccoli is tender. Puree in a blender and set aside.

4. Blanch the broccoli rabe flowers in boiling water for 1 minute. Drain.

5. Cook the gnocchi gently in abundant boiling salted water until they float to the surface. Drain well.

6. Spoon the sauce onto individual plates and cover with a bed of the broccoli rabe flowers. Arrange the gnocchi on top and sprinkle with the shaved pecorino.

SERVES 6

Lasagne verdi Bolognese

GREEN LASAGNE WITH BOLOGNESE SAUCE

An innovation that met with great success at Mezzaluna was replacing
the traditional ricotta cheese between the layers of lasagna with a creamy
béchamel. Our rendition of this classic dish from the Emilia-Romagna region
has been among our best-sellers from the day the restaurant opened.

BOLOGNESE SAUCE

3 ounces dried porcini mushrooms, soaked for 1 hour in lukewarm water

1 pound ground beef

½ pound ground veal

½ cup extra-virgin olive oil

2 celery stalks, chopped

1 carrot, peeled and chopped

1 medium onion, chopped

2 garlic cloves, chopped

1 cup Mezzaluna Tomato Sauce (page 73)

3 tablespoons tomato paste

1 cup dry red wine

2 cups beef broth

2 bay leaves

1 sprig of fresh rosemary, leaves chopped

Fine sea salt and freshly ground black pepper

4 sheets Spinach Pasta (page 93)

4 cups Béchamel Sauce (recipe follows)

2½ cups grated Parmesan cheese

1. Drain the porcini mushrooms, chop coarsely, and set aside.

2. In a skillet, sauté the beef and veal for a few minutes over high heat, breaking up with a wooden spoon. Drain off as much liquid as possible. Set aside.

3. In a large saucepan, heat the olive oil. Add the celery, carrot, and onion and cook for a few minutes over medium heat. Add the garlic and sauté until it is lightly golden, a minute or so longer. Add the meat and mix well. Stir in the tomato sauce, tomato paste, and red wine and cook over high heat for a few minutes, until somewhat reduced. Add the beef broth, bay leaves, rosemary, and porcini mushrooms. Reduce the heat and simmer for 2½ hours, adding more beef broth if necessary. Add salt and pepper to taste.

4. Parboil each lasagna sheet in abundant boiling salted water for 2 minutes. Retrieve with a skimmer and rinse under cold running water. Spread the sheets on a dry kitchen towel and brush both sides with olive oil to prevent sticking.

5. Preheat the oven to 350°F.

6. Grease an 8 × 13 × 2-inch lasagne pan and cover the bottom with ⅔ cup of béchamel sauce. Cover with a sheet of pasta, then add ⅔ cup of béchamel, ⅔ cup of meat sauce, and ⅔ cup of Parmesan. Repeat the procedure 2 more times, ending with the fourth pasta sheet. Cover the top layer completely with béchamel and add a dollop of meat sauce. Top with grated Parmesan cheese and bake for 30 minutes, or until browned and bubbling.

SERVES 6

BÉCHAMEL SAUCE

4 tablespoons (½ stick) unsalted butter	Fine sea salt and freshly ground black pepper
1 cup all-purpose flour	Pinch of nutmeg
1 quart milk, scalded	

Melt the butter in a large saucepan. Add the flour, stirring with a wire whisk. When it is blended and smooth, add the milk and cook over a low flame for 6 or 7 minutes, whisking continuously, or until very thick. Season with salt, pepper, and nutmeg.

MAKES APPROXIMATELY 4 CUPS

Tortelli di zucca con salsa rosa

PUMPKIN TORTELLI WITH PINK SAUCE

*Pumpkin is one of my favorite vegetables and this dish made its debut
at Mezzaluna on our very first menu in 1984. Though pumpkin is generally served
with a butter and sage sauce, I found that the combination of sweet-savory flavors,
which date back to the Renaissance, is particularly enhanced by our pink sauce, which
balances the sweetness of the pumpkin and amaretti cookies. A 4 ½-pound pumpkin
should yield about 2 ¾ pounds of flesh once peeled and seeded.*

---

1 4½-pound pumpkin

4 ounces *Mostarda di Cremona*
or other mixed-fruit chutney with
mustard seeds

2 ounces crushed amaretti
cookies (about 6)

1 teaspoon plum jam

Grated rind of ½ lemon

1 cup grated Parmesan cheese

Pinch of nutmeg

Fine sea salt and freshly
ground black pepper

1 recipe Basic Pasta Dough
(page 79)

PINK SAUCE

1 cup Mezzaluna Tomato Sauce
(page 73)

4 tablespoons (½ stick)
unsalted butter

½ cup heavy cream

---

1. Preheat the oven to 350° F.

2. Wash and seed the pumpkin. Cut it in ¼-inch slices, arrange on a baking
sheet, and bake for 20 to 25 minutes, until tender. When cool, peel the pumpkin
and pass through a food mill or ricer. Transfer to a food processor and combine
with the *Mostarda di Cremona*, amaretti cookies, plum jam, lemon rind, ½ cup
of Parmesan cheese, the nutmeg, and salt and pepper to taste. Process for a few
seconds until well blended. Transfer the filling to a bowl, cover, and allow it to
rest for a few hours.

3. Divide the pasta dough into 4 portions and place on a slightly floured work
surface. Roll with a rolling pin or through a pasta machine to produce thin pasta
layers approximately one-sixteenth inch thick.

4. To prepare half-moon tortelli, spoon the filling by half tablespoons in a row down the center of each pasta sheet. Fold the sheets in half lengthwise. Press down around the dots of filling and cut the half moons by placing half of a round ravioli or cookie cutter over the area containing the filling.

5. Gently cook the tortelli in abundant boiling salted water for 3 to 4 minutes. Using a strainer or a skimmer, transfer to a serving dish.

6. Place the tomato sauce in a strainer set over a bowl and drain off the liquid, discarding the solids. In the top of a double boiler, combine the liquid with the butter and heavy cream and cook over simmering water for 10 minutes.

7. Pour the sauce over the cooked tortelli and sprinkle with the remaining Parmesan cheese.

SERVES 6

Ravioli con porcini e tartufi

RAVIOLI WITH PORCINI MUSHROOMS AND TRUFFLES

*When fresh porcini mushrooms are available, do seek them out—there
is nothing more flavorful. This recipe was introduced to Mezzaluna by my chef
Paolo Casagranda, who comes from the Trento area in northern Italy, renowned
for the best porcini mushrooms. If fresh porcini are not available, you can
substitute a blend of dry porcini and fresh portobello mushrooms.*

4 tablespoons extra-virgin olive oil	2½ cups fresh ricotta cheese
2 garlic cloves, chopped	½ cup grated Parmesan cheese
½ pound fresh porcini or portobello mushrooms	1 egg yolk
	1 tablespoon truffle paste
1 ounce dry porcini mushrooms, soaked in warm water for 20 minutes and drained	Pinch of nutmeg
	1 recipe Basic Pasta Dough (page 79)
2 tablespoons chopped fresh Italian parsley	4 tablespoons (½ stick) unsalted butter
Fine sea salt and freshly ground black pepper	12 fresh sage leaves

1. Heat the oil in a saucepan. Add the garlic and sauté over medium heat until
lightly golden, a minute or two. Add the fresh mushrooms and sauté for 3 to 4
minutes, until slightly softened, then add the dry porcini and simmer over low
heat for 10 minutes. Sprinkle with a tablespoon of parsley and season with salt
and pepper. Allow to cool.

2. Transfer the mushrooms to a food processor. Add the ricotta, Parmesan, egg
yolk, truffle paste, nutmeg, and remaining parsley. Process until well blended.

3. Roll out the pasta dough on a floured work surface or pass through a pasta
machine set on the last setting. Stretch the pasta very thin, less than one-
sixteenth of an inch thick. Cut the dough into 2 equal pieces. Place one sheet on
a work surface and brush with cold water. Stuff the ravioli by dotting half tablespoons of the filling 2 inches apart on the pasta layer. Cover with the second
layer, molding the ravioli by pressing around the filling with your fingers. Cut

between the rows of filling with a pastry cutter to make individual raviolis.

4. In a small saucepan, melt the butter over medium-low heat. Continue to cook until it is nut-colored. Add the sage leaves and keep warm.

5. In the meantime, gently cook the ravioli in abundant boiling salted water. Using a slotted spoon or skimmer, transfer the cooked ravioli to a serving dish. Drizzle the browned butter over the ravioli and serve.

SERVES 6

Pizza

and

Focaccia

✳

*P*IZZA, OF COURSE, is not an American invention. Though it dates back over 2,500 years to the times when southern Italy was a Greek colony, it was in the nineteenth century that pizza as we know it today first appeared on the Neapolitan scene. A local baker, experimenting with an exotic New World import, the tomato, came up with the idea of combining it with the native flat bread. To this day, the narrow streets of Naples showcase the best pizzerias in the world. Among them, the very first pizza shop on record, the Port Alba, founded in 1738, flourishes to this day. ✹ Naples's contribution to the culinary world has become one of the most widely eaten foods on the planet. But for the most part, the pizzas around the globe are a great departure from authentic Neapolitan pizza. As any Italian will tell you, making a pizza is a great art and the artist behind it, the *pizzaiolo*, usually begins learning the trade as a child; pizza making is a time-honored family tradition. ✹ Although the human aspect of preparing a pizza is most important, other factors contribute to the success of achieving an exceptional pizza, namely, the flour, the yeast, the temperature of the oven, and the weather conditions. At Mezzaluna, to make an elastic pizza dough like that in Italy, we combine 75 percent 00 flour, a high-gluten, finely milled flour that has the texture of cake flour, with 25 percent American all-purpose flour. We find that this combination makes a lighter and more digestible pizza. We also use an uncooked tomato sauce so that when the pizza is baked the sauce won't be

cooked twice. Always use a moist brewer's yeast, which is available in specialty stores. As the dough has a life of its own, weather conditions greatly affect it. High humidity is not desirable; ideal conditions call for about 86°F. with a humidity of 35 percent. To reproduce these conditions, allow the dough to rest in a large bowl covered with a damp kitchen towel in a warm, draft-free spot.

It is difficult to reproduce at home the authentic aroma and crispness of a restaurant-made, wood-burning oven pizza. Ideally pizzas should cook only a minute or two at 700°F. However, standard household ovens are unable to attain the high temperature and intensity of a commercial oven, whether electric, wood-burning, or gas-fired. With a heated pizza stone it is possible to approximate the crispy crust produced by a traditional wood-burning oven. These unglazed ceramic bakers are widely available in gourmet houseware stores and come in rectangular and circular shapes; I prefer the circular stones.

Also useful are a wooden peel, the flat paddle used to slide the pizza in and out of the oven, and a rotary cutter to cut the crust quickly and neatly.

And then there is focaccia. My first encounter with focaccia took place during a childhood vacation in the seaside resort of Forte dei Marmi. Carrying a big basket along the beach, Pietro, the man with the "focaccine," soon developed a devoted following; we became addicted to them.

Though no one can agree as to what constitutes a focaccia, it is safe to call it a relative of the pizza. Depending on the region, it comes in almost as many shapes—and has as many names—as pasta. Focaccia is a wonderfully versatile food. You can eat it just with a drizzle of extra-virgin olive oil and fresh herbs. You can top it. You can fill it. My preference is for stuffed focaccia.

At Mezzaluna we serve many different focaccias. A personal favorite is one stuffed with Stracchino, a soft Ligurian cheese, and topped with a drizzle of truffled olive oil. Another popular choice is a focaccia topped with prosciutto di Parma, fontina cheese, and chopped arugula. Just as for pizza, the combinations, and the possibilities, are endless.

Basic Pizza Dough

*This recipe will yield 4 individual-size pizzas, approximately 10 inches
in diameter; each one makes a generous lunch serving or a light appetizer
for two. Extra dough balls can be frozen for up to 2 months.*

2 tablespoons active yeast	**3 cups Italian 00 flour**
1 tablespoon salt	**1 cup all-purpose flour**
1 cup lukewarm (70 to 74° F.) water	**1 tablespoon extra-virgin olive oil**

1. Dissolve the yeast and salt in the lukewarm water.

2. On a large wooden board, combine the 2 flours. With your hands, shape the
flour into a mound. Make a well in the middle of the mound with the back of a
spoon; add the yeast and olive oil gradually and blend all the ingredients together
to make a soft dough. Knead the dough for approximately 15 minutes, until elastic. Set aside to rest for 15 minutes, covered with a damp cotton kitchen towel.

3. Divide the dough into 4 equal portions. Roll each into a ball and place on a
baking sheet, cover with a moist towel, and allow it to rest for 2 to 3 hours at
room temperature, until the dough has doubled in size.

4. Place the pizza stone on the middle or lower oven rack and heat at 450° F. for
25 minutes.

5. On a large floured wooden board, roll the dough into 10-inch circles. With
your fingers, mold a ½-inch rim all the way around the edges.

6. One at a time, place the dough circles on a wooden peel. Cover with the
desired toppings, then slide the pizzas onto the pizza stone. Bake until the crust is
brown and crisp, approximately 20 to 25 minutes.

UNCOOKED TOMATO SAUCE FOR PIZZA

¾ pound (about 4 or 5) fresh plum tomatoes, peeled	**1 teaspoon salt**
	6 fresh basil leaves

Process the tomatoes, salt, and basil leaves in a blender until finely pureed. Set
aside for 1 hour before using.

Pizza Margherita

*Legend has it that in 1889, what has since become the best-known
pizza around the world was named in honor of Queen Margherita di Savoia
by a Neapolitan pizzaiolo named Raffaele Esposito Brandi. Asked by the royal
court to prepare a selection of his celebrated pizzas, he created one that glorified the
colors of the Italian flag, red (tomato), green (basil), and white (mozzarella
cheese), which became the queen's favorite. To this date, a pizzeria in the center of
Naples called Brandi, which claims to be the successor of the famous Raffaele,
continues the tradition of baking the perfect Margherita pie.*

**4 tablespoons Uncooked Tomato
Sauce (page 127)**

3 ounces mozzarella, cubed

Sprinkle of extra-virgin olive oil

4 basil leaves

Spread the tomato sauce over the pizza dough. Top with the mozzarella and
sprinkle with olive oil. Place in the oven and bake until the crust is golden and
the cheese is bubbly, about 20 minutes. Garnish with the basil leaves.

MAKES 1 INDIVIDUAL PIZZA

Pizza ai quattro formaggi

PIZZA WITH FOUR CHEESES

*A great success at Mezzaluna, this classic pizza does not call for tomato sauce.
I like this combination of cheeses because the spicy and sweet flavors are well
balanced, but you can substitute the Italian cheeses of your preference.*

1 ounce fontina cheese, cubed

1 ounce mozzarella cheese, cubed

1 ounce Gorgonzola cheese, cubed

1 ounce provolone cheese, shredded

Cover each quarter of the dough with a different variety of cheese. Slide onto
the pizza stone and bake until the crust is golden and the cheeses are bubbly.

MAKES 1 INDIVIDUAL PIZZA

Pizza Selvatica

PIZZA WITH PESTO AND PIGNOLI NUTS

Mezzaluna's best-selling pizza is my own creation. I wanted to experiment with pesto, famous as a sauce for pasta, in the context of a pizza. The addition of whole pine nuts gives it a delightful crunchiness.

4 tablespoons Uncooked Tomato Sauce (page 127)	3 ounces mozzarella cheese, cubed
2 tablespoons pesto sauce	1 tablespoon pignoli (pine) nuts
	3 fresh basil leaves

Spread the tomato sauce on the pizza dough. Add the pesto and smooth it over the tomato sauce. Top with mozzarella and pignoli nuts. Slide into the oven and bake until the crust is golden brown and the cheese is bubbly. Garnish with basil.

MAKES 1 INDIVIDUAL PIZZA

Pizza Puttanesca

PIZZA WITH SPICY TOMATO, OLIVES, AND CAPERS

In response to endless requests for a pepperoni pizza, which is an American invention, I came up with this spicy pizza. It gets its zest from the famous southern Italian puttanesca *sauce, to which hot red pepper has been added.*

6 tablespoons Uncooked Tomato Sauce (page 127)	15 Ligurian or Niçoise black olives
1 garlic clove, chopped	1 teaspoon Sicilian salt-preserved capers
4 Italian anchovy fillets, packed in oil	1 teaspoon dried hot pepper

Spread the tomato sauce over the pizza dough. Arrange the garlic, anchovies, olives, capers, and hot pepper on top. Slide into the oven and bake until the crust is crisp and golden.

MAKES 1 INDIVIDUAL PIZZA

Pizza con funghi

PIZZA WITH WILD MUSHROOMS

This is a very aromatic and flavorful pizza, particularly suited to the cold months of the year. Use some dry porcini mushrooms to enrich the texture and flavors.

1 tablespoon extra-virgin olive oil

½ garlic clove, chopped

4 ounces fresh wild mushrooms, cleaned and coarsely chopped

½ ounce dried porcini mushrooms, soaked in warm water for 30 minutes

½ tablespoon chopped fresh Italian parsley

4 tablespoons Uncooked Tomato Sauce (page 127)

3 ounces mozzarella cheese, cubed

1. In a skillet, heat the olive oil. Add the garlic and sauté over medium heat until lightly golden. Add the fresh mushrooms and drained porcinis and sauté for 5 to 7 minutes over medium-high heat. Sprinkle with parsley.

2. Spread the tomato sauce over the pizza dough. Top with the mozzarella and add a layer of sautéed mushrooms. Place in the oven and bake until bubbly.

MAKES 1 INDIVIDUAL PIZZA

Pizza bianca con prosciutto e fontina

WHITE PIZZA WITH PROSCIUTTO AND FONTINA CHEESE

Always in great demand at Mezzaluna, this is not a pizza in the traditional sense because it does not have any tomato sauce. It is more in the spirit of a focaccia, sort of a glorified sandwich.

2 ounces fontina cheese, cubed

2 ounces mozzarella cheese, cubed

1 cup coarsely chopped arugula

1 fresh plum tomato, diced

2 tablespoons extra-virgin olive oil

5 paper-thin slices prosciutto

In a bowl, mix the fontina and mozzarella cheeses. Spread on the pizza dough. Slide into the oven and bake until the cheese is bubbly. Then cover the pizza with arugula and tomato and drizzle with olive oil. Top with prosciutto.

MAKES 1 INDIVIDUAL PIZZA

Pizza Marinara

*This is the oldest and simplest pizza. The purists in Naples believe that
there are only two kinds of pizza: the marinara and the margherita, which is
the version with mozzarella cheese. I like the marinara best because I think
it is the most authentic and flavorful. You can also add some anchovies and you
will have a pizza that is typical of the* cucina marinara *of southern Italy.*

**6 tablespoons Uncooked Tomato
Sauce (page 127)**

1 garlic clove, chopped

1 tablespoon chopped fresh oregano

Sprinkle of extra-virgin olive oil

Spread the tomato sauce over the pizza dough. Top with the garlic and oregano.
Sprinkle with olive oil and slide into the oven. Bake until the crust is crisp and
golden brown.

MAKES 1 INDIVIDUAL PIZZA

Basic Focaccia

The rich, yeasty dough of focaccia tastes even better with a drizzle of oil and a sprinkle of fresh herbs or other seasonings; follow your whim. This recipe is also the perfect base for stuffed focaccias; I offer several variations on the following pages.

⅓ cup yeast	2 cups water
¼ cup lukewarm water	1 teaspoon fine sea salt
6½ cups all-purpose flour	2 tablespoons extra-virgin olive oil

1. Combine the yeast with the warm water and stir until dissolved.

2. In a bowl, combine the flour, water, salt, yeast, and 1 tablespoon of the olive oil. Turn out onto a floured board and knead for about 15 minutes, or until very smooth and elastic. Cover the dough with a damp towel and allow it to rest for 5 minutes.

3. Divide the dough into 4 equal portions and shape each into a ball.

4. Stretch the dough in 9-inch baking pans. Cover with a damp kitchen towel and allow to rest for 1½ hours at room temperature, or until it has doubled in size.

5. Turn the dough and with your thumb, press to form little pockets. Brush the focaccias with the remaining tablespoon of olive oil and season with a pinch of salt. Cover with a wet cotton kitchen towel and allow them to rise for about 1 hour.

6. Preheat the oven to 400°F. for at least half an hour before baking the focaccia. Bake the focaccia for 10 to 12 minutes, or until just beginning to color.

MAKES 4 9-INCH FOCACCIAS

The following stuffing recipes will fill one 9-inch focaccia and will serve two.

Caprino e verdure grigliate

GOAT CHEESE AND GRILLED VEGETABLE FOCACCIA

2 zucchini slices, cut lengthwise	½ tablespoon finely chopped fresh Italian parsley
2 eggplant slices, cut very fine	
1 slice red bell pepper	3 ounces fresh goat cheese
1 slice yellow bell pepper	2 ounces Ligurian sun-dried tomatoes, or other oil-packed tomatoes, drained
4 tablespoons extra-virgin olive oil	

1. Marinate the vegetables in the olive oil and parsley for an hour.

2. Grill the vegetables as on page 6 (*Grigliata mista di verdure*).

3. Cut the focaccia crosswise. Spread on the goat cheese, stuff with the grilled vegetables and the sun-dried tomatoes, and bake at 300°F. for 3 to 4 minutes. Sprinkle with extra-virgin olive oil and cut in wedges.

Bresaola, mascarpone, e rucola

SUN-DRIED CURED BEEF, MASCARPONE, AND ARUGULA FOCACCIA

2 ounces mascarpone cheese	3 ounces *bresaola*, thinly sliced
1 tablespoon chopped celery	½ cup chopped arugula
1 tablespoon chopped chives	

Cut the focaccia crosswise. Combine the mascarpone, celery, and chives and mix well. Spread onto the focaccia, add the *bresaola*, and bake at 300°F. for 3 to 4 minutes. Stuff with the arugula and serve.

Stracchino e olio tartufato

STRACCHINO CHEESE AND TRUFFLED OIL FOCACCIA

4 ounces stracchino cheese   **2 tablespoons truffled olive oil**

1. Preheat the oven to 300°F.

2. Cut the focaccia crosswise. Spread with stracchino cheese, replace the top, and place in a baking pan. Bake for 3 to 4 minutes, or until the cheese has melted. Sprinkle with the truffled oil, cut into wedges, and serve immediately.

Sopressata, zucchine, pomodori secchi, e provolone

HOT SALAMI, ZUCCHINI, SUN-DRIED TOMATO, AND PROVOLONE FOCACCIA

3 ounces *sopressata* (hot salami), sliced

2 ounces zucchini, finely sliced and grilled

2 ounces Ligurian sun-dried tomatoes, or other oil-packed tomatoes, drained

3 ounces provolone cheese, finely sliced

Cut the focaccia crosswise. Stuff with the *sopressata*, the grilled zucchini, the sun-dried tomatoes, and the provolone. Bake at 300°F. for 3 to 4 minutes. Cut into wedges.

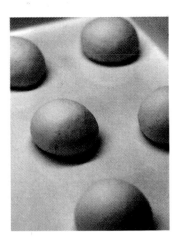

Desserts

✾

A SECONDARY BENEFIT of the healthful, less-filling fare we serve at Mezzaluna is that one nearly always has room for dessert—even if only a rich mouthful or two. For that very reason most of the desserts we serve at Mezzaluna are designed to be eaten with a spoon, making them easy to enjoy *a due*. ✳ Since the day we opened, tiramisù has been the star of the dessert menu, and it seems we can never make enough. Though this dessert has become nearly ubiquitous at restaurants across the country, I modestly contend (and our customers agree) that the sinfully rich and smooth tiramisù served at Mezzaluna is the ultimate version. It is joined by a creamy *panna cotta*, an intensely chocolaty baked pudding, and an almond custard, for those for whom a meal is not complete without a creamy taste of something sweet. ✳ Dessert need not be elaborate. While our grilled fruit salad with zabaglione has its partisans, *affogato al caffè*, steaming espresso served with ice cream and a crisp cookie, is a simple way to end the meal on a sweet note. *"Dulcis in fundo!"* as the Latins said. ✳ I also share here some of the drinks that we've had on the menu, including our ever-popular iced tea.

Stuffed Peaches Dede

This dessert, which I named for my mother, brings back memories of my childhood and summertime, when yellow peaches are at their peak. The most rare and delicious peach, the del poret, is found in the Piedmont region. It is shaped like a lemon and breaks easily in half when pressured with the fingers.

4 large yellow peaches	1 egg yolk
¾ cup crushed amaretti cookies (about 9)	1 tablespoon unsweetened cocoa powder
1 tablespoon ground almonds	1 cup white wine
3 tablespoons granulated sugar	2 tablespoons raw brown sugar

1. Preheat the oven to 350°F.

2. Wash the peaches and pat dry. Cut them in half, remove the pit, and remove a small portion of the pulp with a spoon, creating a cavity.

3. In a bowl, combine the peach pulp, amaretti cookies, almonds, sugar, egg yolk, and cocoa powder. Place in a food processor and mix for a few seconds until smooth.

4. Fill the cavity of each peach with the mixture and arrange them in a 9 × 13-inch baking dish, filling side up. Pour the wine over the peaches, sprinkle with the brown sugar, and bake for 25 minutes. Let the peaches cool and serve at room temperature.

SERVES 4

Bavarese di melone con salsa al kiwi, ananas, e lampone

BAVARIAN CREAM OF MELON WITH KIWI, PINEAPPLE,
AND RASPBERRY SAUCE

This delicate and refreshing dessert is a classic at La Scaletta
restaurant in Milan. Though it is in the tradition of French pâtisserie, the
name "Bavarian cream" pays tribute to the region where so many French
chefs honed their skills at the court of the Wittelsbach princes.

1 pound ripe cantaloupe	½ cup heavy cream, whipped
¾ cup confectioners' sugar	2 kiwifruit, peeled and quartered
2½ gelatin sheets	½ small pineapple, peeled and cored
Juice of 1 lemon	½ cup fresh raspberries

1. Peel and seed the melon. Combine with the sugar in a food processor and process until finely pureed. Transfer to a bowl.

2. In a small saucepan, dissolve the gelatin in 3 tablespoons of warm water and allow it to absorb the liquid. Place over a pan of simmering water and heat until the gelatin is completely dissolved.

3. Stir the gelatin into the melon puree and add the lemon juice. Cool slightly, then fold in the whipped cream. Pour the Bavarian mixture into 4 6-ounce molds and refrigerate for 2 hours.

4. In a blender, combine the kiwifruit, 1 teaspoon of sugar, and 1 teaspoon of lemon juice. Process and set aside. Repeat this procedure with the pineapple and raspberries, reserving each separately.

5. Unmold the Bavarians onto individual plates and surround with dollops of the 3 fruit sauces.

SERVES 4

Macedonia di frutta gratinata allo zabaione

GRILLED FRUIT SALAD WITH ZABAGLIONE SAUCE

Zabaglione, in one version or another, is savored in every region of Italy.
It originated in the 1600s at the court of Savoia in Piedmont, where a chef added
sugar and marsala wine to a beaten egg yolk, thus creating a smooth and very
nutritive cream. I prefer to use vin Santo, a sweet Italian dessert wine.
Zabaglione is a perfect sauce for fresh fruits.

3 egg yolks

¼ cup granulated sugar

2 ½ tablespoons marsala wine

¼ cup sliced strawberries

¼ cup raspberries

½ pear, sliced

1 banana, sliced on the diagonal

1 kiwifruit, peeled and sliced

2 papaya slices

2 tablespoons vin Santo or
1 tablespoon marsala wine

1 teaspoon confectioners' sugar

1 pint vanilla ice cream (optional)

1. In a copper pot, whisk the egg yolks and granulated sugar until white and creamy. Gradually add the 2½ tablespoons marsala wine, beating continuously until the mixture is well combined. Place the bowl over a saucepan of simmering water and cook over medium heat, beating constantly, until the texture is creamy and thick; do not allow it to cook. Pour into a clean bowl.

2. Preheat the broiler.

3. Arrange the fruit in an ovenproof glass baking dish. Sprinkle the fruit with vin Santo or marsala and top with the hot zabaglione sauce. Sprinkle with the confectioners' sugar. Place under the broiler for 30 seconds, or until the zabaglione begins to brown.

4. Serve immediately, topped with a scoop of vanilla ice cream if you wish.

SERVES 4 TO 6

Budino al caffè della "Nonna Lavinia"

ESPRESSO PUDDING "GRANDMA LAVINIA"

*This is a very simple and refreshing dessert that has been served
by my wife's family for generations. It is a very pleasant substitute for
a cup of coffee at the end of a meal. It is made in a mold lined with
caramelized sugar and is very attractive when unmolded.*

2 cups brewed espresso, cooled	1 teaspoon fresh lemon juice
5 tablespoons plus ⅓ cup sugar	1 tablespoon water
5 eggs, beaten	1½ cups whipped cream

1. Combine the cooled espresso and 5 tablespoons of sugar in a mixing bowl and mix well. Add the beaten eggs, one at a time, and mix well.

2. Place the remaining ⅓ cup of sugar, the lemon juice, and the water in a small heavy saucepan. Cook over medium-high heat until the mixture turns a pale caramel color. Immediately pour the caramel into a shallow, 10-inch ring mold, tilting it in all directions to distribute the caramel over the bottom and sides. Continue to tilt until the caramel has hardened. Let the mold cool for 30 minutes.

3. Preheat the oven to 350°F.

4. Pour the coffee mixture into the mold and place the mold in a larger pan filled with enough hot water to come halfway up the sides of the mold. Bake for 1 hour, until the pudding is set and a toothpick inserted in the center comes out dry.

5. Allow the pudding to cool for 1 hour, then unmold onto a serving plate. (If not serving immediately, cover and refrigerate.)

6. Fill the center with the whipped cream and serve.

SERVES 6

Bonet

BITTER CHOCOLATE PUDDING

This traditional dessert from the Piedmont region in Italy takes its name from the copper mold in which it is cooked. A version from the Langhe region uses the cream from the top of the milk, but I prefer this lighter rendition prepared with milk.

2¼ cups sugar	1 quart milk, lukewarm
6 eggs	1 tablespoon rum or dark rum
1 cup crushed amaretti cookies (about 12)	1 cup water
3 tablespoons unsweetened cocoa powder	Fresh strawberries, for garnish
	Whipped cream, for garnish

1. In a bowl, beat ¾ cup of sugar with the eggs until thick. Add the amaretti cookies, cocoa powder, milk, and rum and whisk until smooth and creamy.

2. Preheat the oven to 250°F.

3. In a heavy-bottomed saucepan, combine the water and remaining 1½ cups of sugar. Bring to a boil over medium-high heat and cook for about 20 minutes, until the sugar turns golden brown and creamy. Watch carefully as the sugar begins to color to prevent it from burning.

4. Pour the caramelized sugar into 8 6-ounce round molds and allow to cool. Fill the molds with the chocolate pudding and place in a large baking pan. Fill the pan with enough boiling water to come halfway up the sides of the molds and place in the oven. Bake for 40 minutes. Remove from the oven and allow the puddings to cool.

5. Unmold the puddings onto dessert plates and serve with strawberries and whipped cream.

SERVES 8

Tiramisù

Whether you translate this recipe's name as "lift me up" or "cheer me up," this much-loved dessert will do the trick. What has now become a very popular dessert in the United States was probably first served by restaurateur Alfredo Beltrame at his famous restaurant, Toulá, in the town of Treviso, though its origin could be Venetian. I began serving tiramisù in 1984 and I think Mezzaluna played a significant role in spreading the word about this dessert. As usually happens with very popular dishes, there are now many variations. Many people think ours is the best; I leave it to your palate to decide.

6 eggs, separated	6 cups brewed espresso, cooled
¾ cup sugar	⅓ cup coffee liqueur, such as Kahlúa
7 ounces mascarpone cheese	2 tablespoons unsweetened
½ cup heavy cream	cocoa powder
36 ladyfingers	

1. Combine the egg yolks and sugar in a mixing bowl and beat until you have obtained a creamy thick texture, 4 to 6 minutes. Gradually add the mascarpone. Chill for 10 minutes.

2. In a bowl, beat the egg whites until they are frothy. Gently fold the whites into the chilled mascarpone mixture. Whip the cream until it is stiff and slowly fold into the mascarpone.

3. Line the bottom of an 8 × 12 × 2-inch rectangular glass baking dish with half of the ladyfingers. Combine the cooled coffee and liqueur in a measuring cup. Moisten the ladyfingers with the coffee but do not oversoak them. Spoon a layer of the mascarpone mixture onto the ladyfingers. Add another layer of moistened ladyfingers, followed by the remaining mascarpone mixture. Chill for about 1 hour. Before serving, sprinkle with the cocoa powder.

SERVES 8

Torta di ricotta

RICOTTA CHEESE CAKE WITH STRAWBERRY SAUCE

*I have always loved the texture of traditional American cheesecake. The main
ingredient of my "Italianized" version is ricotta cheese, which produces a smoother
and fuller-flavored cake. An accompaniment of fresh strawberry or raspberry
puree adds a sweet counterpart that is very refreshing.*

DOUGH

4 cups all-purpose flour

½ cup sugar

1 cup (2 sticks) butter, softened

2 egg yolks

2 whole eggs

1 teaspoon vanilla extract

Zest of ½ lemon

1 teaspoon baking soda

FILLING

2 egg yolks

⅓ cup sugar

4 tablespoons (½ stick) butter,
softened

Zest of ½ lemon

1 teaspoon vanilla extract

10 ounces ricotta cheese

1 teaspoon honey

1 teaspoon baking soda

2 egg whites, lightly beaten

SAUCE

1 cup strawberries

Juice of 1 lemon

2 tablespoons sugar

1. To make the dough, pour the flour on a large work surface. In a bowl, blend
the sugar and butter with your hands. Add the egg yolks, whole eggs, vanilla,
lemon zest, and baking soda. Combine with the flour, mixing quickly with your
hands as to not overwork the dough. If the dough is too sticky, add a bit more
flour. Place the dough ball in plastic wrap and allow it to rest overnight in the
refrigerator.

2. The next day, place the dough ball on a floured work surface and, with a
rolling pin, roll it to ⅛ inch thick. Transfer the dough to the 9-inch tube pan,
pressing onto the bottom and up the sides. Set aside.

3. Preheat the oven to 250° F.

4. In a bowl, combine the egg yolks, sugar, soft butter, lemon zest, and vanilla

with an electric mixer. Add the ricotta cheese, honey, and baking soda, and combine gently with a rubber spatula. In a separate bowl, beat the egg whites to stiff peaks. Gently fold the egg whites into the filling and mix very gently.

5. Pour the filling into the prepared pan and bake for $2\frac{1}{2}$ hours. Cool on a rack for 30 minutes, then chill until ready to serve.

6. To make the sauce, puree the fresh strawberries, lemon juice, and sugar in a blender. Strain the puree and chill for at least 30 minutes.

7. Serve the cheesecake in slices topped with a ladleful of sauce.

SERVES 6 TO 8

Biancomangiare con salsa al cioccolato amaro

ALMOND AND VANILLA PUDDING WITH BITTER CHOCOLATE SAUCE

This is a very old dessert, dating back to the Middle Ages,
when it was very popular. Its name is a reference to the mostly white
ingredients, among them almonds, that were introduced to Sicily
by the Arabs during their occupation of southern Italy.

1½ cups (6 ounces) blanched almonds	½ cup sugar
¼ cup (1 ounce) skinned bitter almonds	1 teaspoon vanilla extract
¾ cup warm water	⅓ ounce gelatin, dissolved in water for 5 minutes
Grated rind of ½ lemon	1 tablespoon Grand Marnier
1⅔ cups milk	4½ ounces bitter chocolate, finely chopped or grated

1. With a mortar and pestle or in a food processor, grind both kinds of almonds to a fine paste.

2. In a bowl, combine the warm water and the lemon rind. Add the almond paste, blend thoroughly, and set aside to rest for 1 hour. Strain the almond milk mixture through a sieve and discard the solids.

3. In a saucepan, combine ⅓ cup of milk, the sugar, and the vanilla and bring to a boil over low heat, whisking continuously; add the dissolved gelatin and whisk for a few seconds. Remove from the heat and add the almond liquid, the Grand Marnier, and the remaining 1⅓ cups milk. Mix very well and pour into a 10-inch mold or bowl; refrigerate for 3 hours.

4. Melt the chocolate in the top of a double boiler over simmering water. Stir until very smooth.

5. Unmold the puddings and serve with some of the melted chocolate drizzled over each serving.

SERVES 6 TO 8

Panna cotta all'Amaretto

COOKED CREAM MOLDS WITH AMARETTO

Panna cotta *literally means "cooked cream." Of French origin, this dessert*
was first introduced to the Piedmont and Ligurian regions, which border France.
To make the dessert even more special, you can coat the inside of the molds with
caramelized sugar (page 142) in the style of a French crème caramel.

2 cups heavy (whipping) cream	**1 package (2 sheets) unflavored gelatin**
1 cup milk	
¾ cup sugar	**1 cup pureed strawberries, raspberries, or boysenberries, or other fresh fruit, for garnish (optional)**
½ cup finely chopped toasted hazelnuts	
3 tablespoons Amaretto	

1. In a saucepan, combine the heavy cream, milk, and sugar. Mix with a wire whisk and cook over a low flame.

2. Add the hazelnuts and Amaretto and continue whisking. Add the gelatin, bring to a boil, and cook for a few seconds. Pour immediately into individual ramekins and refrigerate for at least 4 hours.

3. Unmold the *panna cotta* and serve with a few spoonfuls of pureed berries or fresh fruit if desired.

SERVES 6 TO 8

Affogato al caffè

VANILLA ICE CREAM WITH HOT ESPRESSO

*As a substitute for plain coffee or espresso at the end of a meal, this
dessert is always well received and takes next to no time to prepare. Affogato
means "drowned," and many people believe that adding a "drowning"
scoop of ice cream to strong espresso tames the effect of the caffeine.*

1 cup brewed espresso	2 ounces bittersweet chocolate
3 scoops vanilla ice cream	(optional), melted over simmering
1 pirouette cookie	water

Pour the hot espresso over the ice cream and decorate with a pirouette cookie.
If you wish, pour melted chocolate over the ice cream.

SERVES 1

Paciugo alle amarene

THREE-FLAVOR SUNDAE WITH SOUR CHERRIES

In the Ligurian dialect, paciugo *means "a muddy mix."
This dessert was invented in a bar in the trendy resort of Portofino.*

4 scoops vanilla ice cream	½ cup sour cherries in syrup
4 scoops chocolate ice cream	½ cup whipped cream
4 scoops raspberry ice cream or sorbet	

In each of 4 tall glasses, layer a scoop of vanilla, chocolate, and raspberry ice
cream. Top each with 2 tablespoons of cherries and syrup and a dollop of
whipped cream.

SERVES 4

Seasonal Fruit Cocktails

In addition to more traditional aperitifs, at the restaurant we also
offer fruit-based wine drinks—a different one for each season. These refreshing
coolers combine pureed ripe fruit with cold Prosecco, a sparkling wine from
the Veneto region that is Italy's version of champagne. Each of the cocktail recipes
below yields four 4-ounce servings, but the basic formula is easily multiplied up;
just use a ratio of 1 part fruit puree to 3 parts chilled wine.

BASIC FRUIT PUREE

Try to start with chilled ingredients if you will be using the fruit puree
immediately. And be sure to use fully ripened fruit for the sweetest flavor.
Do not overprocess the puree; it should have a bit of texture.

½ **pound cleaned, peeled fruit** (**strawberries, peaches, pears, etc.**)	1 **teaspoon fresh lemon juice** 1 **tablespoon sugar**

Cut the fruit into large chunks and place in the bowl of a food processor. Process
for 15 seconds, then add the lemon juice and sugar to taste and puree until barely
smooth. Force the puree through a fine strainer, pressing the pulp through with
a wooden spoon. Chill thoroughly until ready to use.

MAKES APPROXIMATELY ½ CUP

Botticelli

SPRING

½ **cup strawberry puree** : 1½ **cups chilled Prosecco**

Place the strawberry puree in a carafe. Slowly add the wine and stir to blend.
Pour into 4 well-chilled goblets and serve.

Bellini

SUMMER

½ cup white peach puree : **1½ cups chilled Prosecco**

Place the peach puree in a carafe. Slowly add the wine and stir to blend. Pour into 4 well-chilled goblets and serve.

Tiziano

AUTUMN

½ cup red grape juice (see Note) : **1½ cups chilled Prosecco**

Place the grape juice in a carafe. Slowly add the wine and stir to blend. Pour into 4 well-chilled goblets and serve.

NOTE: Unsweetened grape juice is available at many farmer's markets and health food stores; to make your own, pass approximately ½ pound of sweet red grapes through a food mill or fine mesh strainer.

Canaletto

WINTER

½ cup pear puree : **1½ cups chilled Prosecco**

Place the pear puree in a carafe. Slowly add the wine and stir to blend. Pour into 4 well-chilled goblets and serve.

Mezzaluna Iced Tea

*Since brewing tea is an Anglo-Saxon art, we were challenged
to give ours a Mediterranean touch. The response was terrific
and it has become a signature item at Mezzaluna.*

3 teaspoons Earl Grey tea	Zest of ½ lemon
2 teaspoons Darjeeling tea	4 large strawberries
1 teaspoon black currant (cassis) tea	Fresh mint leaves, for garnish
½ cup sugar	Orange slices, for garnish
Juice of 1 orange	

Boil ½ gallon of water. Add the tea and let it brew for 5 to 6 minutes. Do not let
it stand too long as it will become bitter. Strain the tea and transfer to a large
carafe. Add the sugar, orange juice, lemon zest, and strawberries. Stir and allow it
to cool for an hour at room temperature. Discard the strawberries and lemon zest
and refrigerate. Serve with mint leaves and an orange slice in a tall glass.

SERVES 8

Mail-Order Directory

ANDRONICO'S MARKET
1200 Irving Street
San Francisco, CA 94122
(800) 522-4438

BALDUCCI AND CO.
11-02 Queens Plaza South
Long Island City, NY 11101
(800) 225-3822

CORTI BROTHERS
5810 Folsom Boulevard
Sacramento, CA 95819
(916) 736-3800

DEAN & DELUCA
560 Broadway
New York, NY 10012
(800) 221-7714

FERRARA
195 Grand Street
New York, NY 10013
(212) 226-6150

G. B. RATTO & CO.
821 Washington Street
Oakland, CA 94607
(800) 325-3483

TODARO BROTHERS
555 Second Avenue
New York, NY 10016
(212) 679-7766

VIVANDE, INC.
2125 Fillmore Street
San Francisco, CA 94115
(415) 346-4430

WILLIAMS-SONOMA
Mail Order Dept., P.O. Box 7456
San Francisco, CA 94120
(415) 421-4242

ZINGERMAN'S DELICATESSEN
422 Detroit Street
Ann Arbor, MI 48104
(313) 663-3400

Index